Heart Activation
TOOLKIT

A Combination Book and
Workbook Designed to
Equip You with the Tools
and Techniques to
Activate Your Heart and
Discover True,
Unconditional
Self-Love

Tami Jean

This book is intended as a reference volume only, not as a medical manual. The information given here is designed to inspire and inform. It is not intended as a substitute for any treatment that may have been prescribed by your doctor. If you suspect that you have a medical problem, we urge you to seek competent medical help.

Printed in the United States of America
Published in Hellertown, PA
Cover and interior design by Tami Jean Lowe
ISBN 979-8-89420-062-0
For more information or to place bulk orders, contact the author or the publisher at
Jennifer@BrightCommunications.net.

Bright
COMMUNICATIONS

To my sons

Contents

Introduction

I was born Tami Jean Wimmer, August 29, 1973, in Apple Valley, California, to parents who were doing everything "right." Now retired elementary school teachers, my parents grew up in typical American households, are college educated, and were checking off all the right boxes.

My father spent time before marrying in his late thirties exploring the country. As a teacher, he spent his summers driving his Porsche across America, exploring all of the different landscapes and seeing all the sites. Born and raised in Bethlehem, Pennsylvania, he lived a full life as a dance teacher, camp director, and art teacher, on top of teaching his fifth-grade class until retirement.

One thesis away from his doctorate in education, my father is a perpetual teacher. Anything we ever did was overtoned with how-to's. As a kid I hated this, but now I realize how much he gave to me with his many boring lessons.

On one of my fathers many trips, he followed a map created by one of his students. He was directed to travel Route 66 from Chicago to Los Angeles. On this journey, he came to a tiny town in the Mojave Desert called Barstow. He fell in love with this town and ended up taking a job and moving there. A couple years later, he was introduced to my mother. Despite the crippling homesickness, she married him and moved out to California. They worked for many years in the same school district, both retiring from there. After 11 years, they divorced, and my father moved back to Pennsylvania.

My mother, who stayed in California and remarried the love of her life, is a kind, conservative soul, formed by a controlling father and victimized mother. While doing a card reading for my mom, I asked what she wanted to know. At 73 years old, she wanted to know when she would feel comfortable in her own skin. That has never left me. Every card pulled for her was about authenticity. I am grateful for the lessons I've learned from her about being true to myself and my dreams.

As a child, I was a burden and often in the way, but as an adult. I am a strong authentic woman. and my mother is proud of who I have become.

The experience I have gained for this book was learned along a long, winding, and broken road, through a childhood where I did not receive the love and acceptance I needed and deserved, two failed marriages and two long-term relationships that taught me about love, and what love is not and through my many "bad choices" that were only lessons unfolding. I have grown into a person who is confident in who she is today. This journey is still full of ups and downs, but such is life. Without the downs, we wouldn't have the ups. Without the dark, we wouldn't have the light. And without the pain, we wouldn't appreciate the pleasure of life.

As a coach, I have learned that every coach needs a coach. We are on this journey together, and I learn alongside you through this program. As I teach you, you will teach me. We are all continuously evolving and morphing into who we are meant to be. As a caterpillar becomes a butterfly, during the chrysalis phase, it will experience much pain and discomfort. The pain and discomfort strengthen those muscles to be able to fly with our new wings!

I was inspired to bring together the many tools and techniques I have gained along this journey and share them with you. This will be an ever-evolving process as I continuously grow and evolve myself. But now is the time. This is my one step. Thank you for joining me on this journey.

Namaste'

Recognitions

Each journey begins with a single step. –Lao Tzu

Thank you to all of my coaches and teachers who supported me, and some who continue to support me, to get to this place of being able to help other women like me.

To my most important teacher: Thank you for coming to this Earth and giving me the opportunity to suffer so I could bloom into the woman I have become. We loved, we loathed, and in time we found peace. Thank you for the biggest blessings I have, our sons. May you rest in peace.

To Richard, Harley, and Dalton, the truest loves of my life, I am more grateful for you than you could ever imagine. Thank you for keeping me grounded and real. Thank you for challenging me and for accepting me for who I am and forgiving me for the hurt I caused you during my difficult times. And thank you for the daughters you have given me along the way. I love you all more than life itself.

Thanks to my lifelong friends who have put up with all my ups and downs and to my family who shaped me into who I am today. Thank you to my many clients who showed me the many vast relationships between women and how important they are. And to all my exes, thank you for giving me the opportunity to learn what love is not, which taught me what love is. Thank you for showing me the broken pathway to finding True Unconditional Self-Love. I wouldn't be here without you.

Be grateful for the lessons and leave the past where it belongs.

Heart Activation

Several years back, the concept of Heart Activation came to me as an idea for a program. I realized that through discovering all of these seemingly tiny tools and my strong desire to learn them all, I was able to bumble my way down the path of life, healing my trauma a little bit at a time. As I went along, I gathered tool by tool, technique by technique, sometimes overwhelmed at all the opportunities to learn. I had to reel myself in and prioritize what I wanted to learn first and build from there.

Someone suggested to me that I focus on one tool at a time, learning how to use each tool properly and become very familiar with it before moving onto the next. Because I am always excited to learn new tools and get bored easily, it was difficult for me to do that. More than once in my life I've been called a "seed planter." As I learn new things, I am generally very excited about them and tend to share with people who I come into contact with. What I share is often brand new to the other person or they may have heard about it but didn't really know or understand it. I am easily able to create an opportunity for them to learn and grow.

As I began to tap into astrology, I learned of a dwarf planet called Chiron. Nicknamed "The Wounded Healer," in Greek mythology Chiron was a great healer. An immortal Centaur half man/half horse, Chiron was accidentally hit with a deadly poisonous arrow that he had created and given to Hercules, one of his favorite disciples. Because Chiron could not die, he suffered great pain and spent the rest of his life trying to heal his own wound, and in turn he created medicine that helped many others along the way.

I relate very much to this story, and for those who understand astrology, my Chiron is in my 12th house in Aries. The 12th house represents spirituality. (More on astrological charts in Module 3 Lesson 8.) On the next page, is my personal chart explaining this. This information helped me to understand my strengths, wounds, and weaknesses. Awareness is the key. Understanding this helped me to see why I often felt futile and gave up often, never able to get ahead. But we are able to get ahead, if we choose to do so!

My Personal Chart on Chiron

Chiron - Wounded Healer, inner teacher

Chiron is an asteroid between Saturn and Uranus. Its orbit is very unusual and represents a bridge between material and spiritual worlds.

According to mythology, Chiron was a great healer, wise teacher, and one of the immortal Centaurs. Unfortunately, he was "deadly" injured by a poisonous arrow by Heracles, his favorite disciple. He was suffering in great pain, but he could not die. Finally, he gave up his immortality for the benefit of Prometheus, who was also suffering, and Chiron was sent to the underworld. In the underworld, Zeus had mercy for him, and he raised him to the heaven.

In astrology, Chiron symbolizes our unhealable injuries and incurable trauma. However, if a person, instead of drowning in his own trauma, is able to accept the trauma and help others who are also suffering, and accept that suffering is part of life, then Chiron may be the key to wisdom, or even to some sort of "Initiation Gate."

Chiron in Aries

These people may be traumatized by the fact that despite all their efforts they are not successful because they are not very proactive and assertive; they lack the appropriate dose of healthy aggression that is needed in a competitive society in order to survive competition with those who are too harsh and ruthless. They usually compensate for this with exaggerated activity, but the results never correspond with the effort they put in.

Chiron in the 12th House

These people believe that the world is a place of great suffering and that there is physical and moral misery, illness, violence, and injustice all around us. Even sympathy with suffering people can become unhealable injury because this suffering never ends. These people can react with disgust and resignation, or on the contrary, by helping others because by helping others these people can also heal their own irreparable injury.

As I began to understand this, it empowered me to know that a large part of my purpose on this Earth is to share what I am learning on my own healing journey to help others around me. As I share the tools I learn with others instinctively, I allow them the opportunity to awaken and begin their healing journey as well. My excitement over each and every tool radiates to those I come in contact with.

Along with this realization, I had come to a place in my life with two failed marriages, and now two failed long-term partners. What I learned from the two latter relationships, among other things, was that both of these men were good men who cared for me deeply, but they were not able to open their hearts and let me in.

I desired, required, and deserved more, so as difficult as it was, I left them both behind, not to find another man but to find a way to fall in love with myself. I did not like myself, much less love myself!

My coach at the time recommended I spend some time with myself because I had never done that before.

I recommend you do this. Going through the healing and opportunity to find love within, instead of outside of yourself, will create a major shift in your energy field, in turn creating a shift in the type of energy you attract. This is not a program to help you find love. However, you may discover that finding your true soulmate, lover, and best friend is a "side effect" of this program.

How to Use This Book

First and foremost, I feel it is supremely important that you take this program in bite-size portions giving time for integration.

I do not recommend reading cover to cover or skipping around as I have laid out each tool in meticulous order for your growth. Between each module, I recommend a week of integration time and an Integration-Week Card Reading to gauge where you are at in your process and to get information to empower and encourage you along.

I recommended that you start Lesson 1 three weeks prior to a Full Moon for the lessons to line up properly with the moon phases. (See Moon Phase calendar within the provided QR Code link on page 13.)

Breakdown of Lessons

	1ST LESSON	2ND LESSON	3RD LESSON	INTEGRATION WEEK
MODULE 1	Morning Routine	Crystals Grounding Protection	Cord Cutting Archangels	Integration Card Reading
MODULE 2	Obstacle Breaker Allowing Receiving	Storytelling Karma Dharma	Full Moon Release Ceremony	Integration Card Reading
MODULE 3	New Moon Manifestation Frequencies Affirmations	Natal Chart Astrology	Self-Forgiveness Taking Responsibility	Integration Card Reading
MODULE 4	Inner Child Playtime Acts of Self-Love	Matrix Boundaries Expansion	Relationships Red Flags Love Languages	Integration Card Reading
MODULE 5	Care for the Body	Care for the Mind	Care for the Soul/Spirit	Heart Activation Final Card Reading Celebration

This is intended and designed to be a 20-week process, allowing a week between each module for integration of new lessons.

Included in This Program

- 11-piece toolkit available for only $175 ($225 value)
- 1 complimentary extended card reading (first reading)
- 5 extended card readings at discounted rate (33% off)
- 1 complimentary 30-minute session with me ($60 per hour for any following sessions)
- Email communications for questions or concerns
- 5 Modules
- 15 Lessons ($1500 value)
- 4 Integration Weeks
- 54 new tools to play with ($1,100 value)
- 8 recorded guided meditations ($800 value)
- An Activated Heart ready to Accept and Receive Love (Priceless)
- A New Perspective on Life (Priceless)

$12,500 value

Heart Activation
Toolkit Links

Or go to:

Https://linktr.ee/HeartActivationProgram

Use this QR code to take you to all the tools you will need for this program.
Feel free to contact me for questions or support. You are not alone on this journey!

Journal Pages

Between each lesson, you will find four full journal pages. This is intended to be an interactive workbook. Write in it! Mark it up, jot your feelings, and log your progress. In time, you will be able to look back and see your growth and changes.

You will also find a larger section at the end of this book for journaling.

Another suggestion is not to mark up the book and use a separate journal. Once you are finished with it, share it with someone else you feel may benefit from this program, along with their own journal and pen. Or have a group session with friends or loved ones.

_____

_____

_____

_____

_____

_____

_____

_____

_____

_____

_____

_____

_____

_____

Heart Activation Baseline Card Reading

Beginning with a complimentary Baseline Heart Activation Card Reading, specifically designed for this course, is not necessary, but highly recommended!

Card reading is a beautiful tool in which your Guides and Angels can give you information and insight. They can empower you with knowledge to support you in your journey. This reading will give you an idea of what areas are of most importance for you to focus on your healing journey.

Card readings give me insight and confidence that everything is going to be okay and that I am going in the right direction! They helped me to realize my potential and that my Guides and Angels were there cheering me on and supporting me through the challenging parts of my journey.

Your Heart Activation baseline reading will be done at a distance, not in person. I will say a prayer calling in your energy, Spirit Guides, Guardian Angels, Ancestors, and Ascended Masters to give me information, with only Love and light, through the cards and intuitively. I will take pictures and record the reading on video and audio and email them to you within a week of your request.

Each subsequent reading throughout the course costs $40. Use the QR code to schedule your reading. It will then show on my calendar. If you would prefer a reading on Zoom or in person (if local), please use the contact form in the QR code below.

Heart Activation
Baseline Card
Reading Link

Toolkit

I'm pleased to offer you the opportunity to purchase my recommended tools. All items are created or assembled by me personally. Each is made with Love and infused with Reiki.

I recommend you order and schedule your Heart Activation Baseline Reading at the same time, giving time for delivery of your toolkit, prior to starting lessons. (Suggestion: Order on a Full Moon.)

 Heart Activation Toolkit

Heart Activation Toolkit

Kit includes

Mending Hearts Bookmark and Pen $20
Cord Cutting Crystal Set $15
Chakra Crystal Set $25
Protection Crystal Set $20
Ganesha Mala Beads $75
Smudge Kit $20
Space Cleansing Set Himalayan Sea Salt $20
Uplifting Rose Water $10
Calming Lavender $20
Total $175
($225 value)

Join the Heart Activation Facebook Group

If you are interested in finding more support, I have created a private Facebook group exclusively for this program. I am very cautious with this group, so be sure to answer the group rules or you will not be accepted.

Heart Activation Program Private Facebook Group

Contract with Yourself

The contract that follows is for you, and only you. It is not a commitment to me, but a promise to yourself to follow through with this program. One of the biggest barriers I still run into now and then is follow-through. So, I have designed this contract to be with you and your Higher Self.

How many times have you promised to do something for someone else and given up something you planned to do for you? We make commitments to other people, and we follow through, more often than not, because of that commitment. It is time for you to become reliant unto yourself, putting your own needs above others. Life will always get in the way of your healing journey if you let it.

I want you to be successful in this endeavor because I believe in you! I see your true potential and your value, even though you may not.

Create a weekly time for your lessons. Set all else aside and commit to yourself. You can do this. You DESERVE this! You are WORTH IT!

Contract with Your Higher Self

I, _____, promise to my Higher Self to complete this program. I promise to finish each chapter as instructed, giving the recommended time between lessons, as this will be for my highest and best results.

I promise to take these 20 weeks, committing to self-love and self-care practices, and to be open-minded and open-hearted as to allow my Heart to open.

This is not a commitment to anyone but myself, and I promise to commit to finishing the program and being reliable unto myself.

I agree to avoid, if possible, dating or any relations with the opposite sex during this program because that will give me the best results to finding self-love and activating my heart.

Date: _____/_____/_____

Signature: _____

What is your 'why' for taking this program?

Write where you are currently as you begin this program. In time, you will be able to look back and see your progress.

_____

_____

_____

_____

_____

_____

_____

_____

_____

_____

_____

_____

_____

_____

_____

_____

_____

_____

_____

_____

_____

_____

_____

_____

_____

Module 1
Building Blocks

"As a solid rock is not shaken by the wind, so the wise are not moved by praise or blame."
— Dhammapada, Verse 81

Inner stillness and wisdom form the true foundation that cannot be shaken.

Module 1: Building Blocks
Lesson 1: Creating a Morning Routine

Creating a morning routine is a great tool to start your day in a positive energy. It's a way for you to begin your day showing yourself the Self-Love you deserve. It is also a great foundation for you to build your journey on.

Taking time before you even roll out of bed will help to create a positive energy for the day—energy of gratitude. This may seem simple, or even silly. However, it is a very powerful tool to create a positive energy that can snowball into the rest of your day, and even life! We are very powerful creators, and we must be careful with our thoughts because what we see around us is what we have created with our thoughts.

I struggle with mornings. But, on the days I take the time to visualize what I want to see in my life, express gratitude for even the smallest blessings, affirm what I want, and take at least five deep breaths, I can definitely see the difference in how my days go.

All of the tools I teach in this course have helped me to change my life. Believe me, I am not always Susie Sunshine, and I slip up a lot! But I have seen a clear difference in my life when I use these tools. They have helped me to create a love for myself, a healthier relationship with my friends and family, and brought me a life partner who I never could have dreamed possible! Even if you aren't perfect at this, it will shift things for you. In Module 3 Lesson 9 Part 1, we will discuss forgiveness for those slip ups!

Before Getting Out of Bed

17-Second Visualization

Upon waking, take at least 17 seconds to visualize what you want your life to look like or a specific situation and how you want to see it turn out. Holding a positive thought for at least 17 seconds will create the momentum to bring those thoughts into your reality, or vortex. Your vortex is like the waiting room of reality creation.

I learned this tool from Abraham-Hicks, a well-known inspirational speaker and channeler. Being able to focus our energy for only 17 seconds can change the way our mind creates our reality. According to A-H, our mind is a very powerful creation tool. Taking this seemingly insignificant amount of time to visualize what we want can begin the shift from where we are currently to where we want to be! The link for the full recording is in the main QR Code on page 13.

Gratitude

While still lying in bed, just after the 17-second visualization, think of at least five things you are grateful for.

Gratitude is a high-vibrational energy. (More about vibration and frequency in Module 3 Lesson 7.)

Sometimes it can be difficult to find things to be grateful for. On those days, I focus on even the tiniest things. I express gratitude for my comfortable bed, my microfiber super soft body pillow, my finger and toenails (what a miracle these things truly are!), electricity, and indoor plumbing! There are so many things in our world that we have become accustomed to and take for granted; however, when we think about it, we are so blessed to have all the comforts we do!

When you focus on these small blessings, it will create a snowball effect to attract more positive energy into your matrix (space). Like attracts like. It's as strong as the Law of Gravity, the Law of Attraction will bring the energy you create back to you! Life is not always rainbows and unicorns. I wish it was! However, facing the difficult times with a more positive perspective can change everything! (More on perspective in Module 2 Lesson 2.)

Deep Breathing

After expressing gratitude, take five deep cleansing breaths. Breathe in as deep as you are able to comfortably, holding that breath for four seconds, and releasing that breath, blowing until your lungs are completely empty. Visualize the breath coming into your body as a bright white light energy and blow out any dark energy, imagining dark smoke leaving your body. (More on breathwork in Module 5 Lesson 15.) Breathing in that light energy and releasing any dark energy can help you to start your day in a more positive light energy.

Rose Water

Once you sit up, spray your face from about a foot away with a light mist of pure organic rose water, breathing in that beautiful fragrance. I keep my rose water on my night table so I see it when I sit up.

Rose is known to be a very high vibrational fragrance. Bringing this into your space will help to raise your energetic vibration. Rose vibrates at a natural 320 Hz! Humans sit between 65 and 70 Hz naturally. Adding higher vibrational energy, including scents, music, or frequency, will raise your natural vibration, bringing in a more positive, lighter energy to your body.

Journaling

Journaling is a great tool to help destress, preserve daily memories, or write down dreams or ideas you may have had overnight. Spend at least five minutes writing in your journal while having your morning coffee or tea. You can also write the things and people you are grateful for. This is useful when you are having a bad day to look back on and help you remember what you have to be grateful for.

Assignment

We are creating a foundation for the rest of the program by doing these five very simple techniques. Starting your day in a lighter, more positive energy is going to be a beautiful, strong foundation for you to continue to build on throughout this program.

If you find this difficult, choose one or two of the techniques and build on them over time. Example, take five deep cleansing breaths and express five things you are grateful for each morning before exiting the bed.

Record your experiences in the journaling pages that follow. Feel free to share in the Heart Activation Facebook group if you feel called. (Link to join private group in QR code on page 13.)

Module 1: Building Blocks
Lesson 2: Gathering Tools
Part 1: Understanding Crystals

Crystals have been used for thousands of years to assist in physical, emotional, and spiritual healing, all over the world! For example, Clear Quartz are known to have powered the world long before there was modern electricity. Today they help to power our watches, televisions, and computer screens, among many other things.

Crystals each vibrate at their own unique frequency. Black and darker color crystals vibrate at a lower energetic frequency and the clear and lighter colors vibrate at a higher energetic frequency. Crystals are used in healing sessions, such as Reiki and crystal therapy, often to balance our Chakras.

Chakras make up the energetic field that surrounds our bodies. Another word used for this is your Aura. As you picture your body, visualize an invisible field around you that extends about three feet out. The image on page 31 shows where the Chakras are located in our body. These are the main seven Chakras, though there are several others between, above, and below the body.

Here are some examples of crystals used in Chakra balancing.

- Root Chakra (red): Hematite, Obsidian, Garnet, Red Jasper
- Sacral Chakra (orange): Carnelian, Red Aventurine, Goldstone
- Solar Plexus Chakra (yellow): Tigers Eye, Citrine, Yellow Jade and Jasper, Mookaite
  (Mustard-also comes in varied maroon to yellow)
- Heart Chakra (green): Rose Quartz, Malachite, Serpentine, Green Aventurine

- Throat Chakra (blue): Lapis Lazuli, Turquoise, Aquamarine
- Third Eye Chakra (indigo or purple): Sodalite, Amethyst, Charoite, Lepidolite
- Crown Chakra (violet or white): Clear Quartz, White Jade, Agate, Moonstone

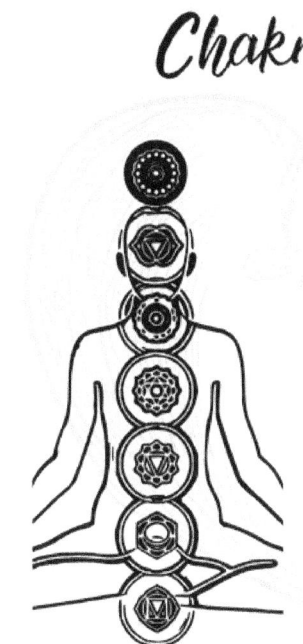

Chakra Chart

CROWN. VIOLET. LOCATED AT TOP OF HEAD. REPRESENTS CONNECTION TO DIVINE, SOURCE, OR GOD.

THIRD EYE. INDIGO. LOCATED JUST ABOVE THE CENTER OF BROWS. REPRESENTS INTUITION. THE STILL, SMALL VOICE.

THROAT. BLUE. LOCATED AT JAWLINE. REPRESENTS SPEAKING OUR TRUTH. OUR AUTHENTICITY.

HEART. GREEN. LOCATED IN CENTER OF BREASTBONE. REPRESENTS LOVE OF SELF, OTHERS, AND THE DIVINE, SOURCE, OR GOD.

SOLAR PLEXUS. YELLOW. LOCATED ABOVE THE NAVAL. REPRESENTS SELF. CORE BEING. "I AM."

SACRAL. ORANGE. LOCATED BELOW THE NAVAL/WOMB AREA. REPRESENTS REPRODUCTION, CREATIVITY.

ROOT. RED. LOCATED AT PUBIC BONE. REPRESENTS FAMILY, ROOTS, WHERE WE CAME FROM.

CHAKRA-BALANCING MEDITATION

At this time, you will listen to the Chakra-Balancing Guided Meditation.

Create a beautiful and quiet space for yourself if you are able at this time or schedule a time very soon for your meditation. Be sure to have uninterrupted time to do this. This is the first of eight custom guided meditations I wrote and recorded with a live Sound Bath just for this program.

This Guided Meditation is intended to assist in balancing your Chakra system. Specially channeled by me just for you.

Record your experience on the following journal pages. Feel free to share in the Heart Activation Facebook group if you feel called. (Link to join private group in QR code on page 13.)

Chakra-Balancing
Guided Meditation

Module 1: Building Blocks
Lesson 2: Gathering Tools
Part 2: Grounding and Protection

Grounding

Because we are all energetic beings and function with electronic signals from the brain, it's important to keep our physical energy grounded, as well as in our homes and buildings. If we don't, we can have symptoms such as:

- Scattered thoughts
- Foggy brain
- Feeling flighty
- Inability to think clearly and make decisions

To make matters worse, many people in our modern society are wearing shoes with rubber soles. This has created an environment full of ungrounded humans. This rubber prevents electromagnetic currents from running through our bodies. The magnetic field of the Earth is intended to keep our energy charged and grounded, and when we don't connect with the Earth, we become depleted and scattered. This is all too common.

Here are some techniques to help you get grounded.

- Walk barefoot in the dirt or grass daily for at least several minutes. Twenty minutes a day is ideal. However, this isn't always possible. Anything will help.
- Wear leather-bottomed shoes whenever possible. (There are many leather shoemakers on Etsy.)
- Keep Root Chakra crystals on your person, whether in your bra, pocket, or in jewelry. Check out my jewelry line Mending Hearts Crystal Therapy here: https://www.mendingheartshealing.com/shop.

- Visualize tree roots growing from either your feet (while standing) or your torso (when sitting) growing from your body down into the Earth. Imagine them going through the Earth into the core and connecting you with the Earth. This is a good way to ground yourself when you are in a public place and can't do any of the other techniques

Using these techniques will help you to balance and stabilize your energetic field and allow you to feel more centered and grounded.

Protection

Along with grounding, it's important to protect your energy and your space. There are many ways you can do this physically and energetically. Here are some examples.

- Carry or wear protection crystals. Black Tourmaline, Hematite, Obsidian, and Tigers Eye [of any color] are often used for protection.
- Imagine an invisible bubble around your body or personal space preventing you from absorbing others emotions and energy or keeping others from stealing your energy, sometimes referred to as energy suckers. This is especially useful if you are empathic, meaning you pick up on other people's emotions or energy easily.
- If you have encountered an energy sucker or can feel residual energy, you can perform what's called a dry bath. Simply use your hands to sweep from your head to your toes and give that negative energy to Mother Earth Gaia, thanking her for taking it from you.
- Call in the Archangels, particularly Archangel Michael because he is the great protector. I like to imagine four archangels holding a security blanket over our home or if I am driving, I imagine they are carrying my car in the security blanket.
- Smudge your space to remove negative or stagnant energy from your home, personal space, or workspace.

My smudge kit (see page 16) includes:

- White sage bundle: removes negative and residual energy
- Pala Santo stick: replaces negative energy with positive love and light energy
- Abalone shell: to lay the Sage and Pala Santo into safely
- Feather: for spreading smoke throughout the space
- Black Tourmaline: absorbs and transmutes negative energy into positive energy
- Selenite: clears space
- Amethyst: brings tranquility
- Clear Quartz: offers supreme healing energy
- Instructions for use and prayer to use during cleansing

These are all suggestions of tools and techniques I have used and love. There are many options available. Find what works best for you.

GROUNDING AND PROTECTION GUIDED MEDITATION

At this time, you will listen to the Grounding and Protection Guided Meditation.
Create a beautiful and quiet space for yourself if you are able at this time or schedule a time very soon for your meditation. Be sure to have uninterrupted time to do this. This is the second of eight guided meditations custom written and recorded with a live Sound Bath just for this program.
This Guided Meditation is intended to assist in grounding your physical body and protecting your energetic body. Specially channeled by me just for you.

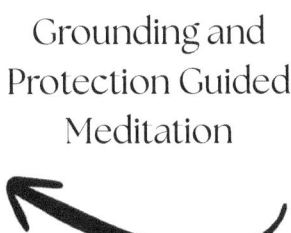

Grounding and Protection Guided Meditation

Assignment

Grounding and protection are tools that can be carried with you throughout your life.

This week, practice using one of each of the grounding and protection techniques. (Or more if you feel called to.)

Record your experience on the following journal pages. Feel free to share in the Heart Activation Facebook group if you feel called. (Link to join private group in QR code on page 13.)

Module 1: Building Blocks
Lesson 3: Cord Cutting

Cord cutting is a very important tool to release, move forward more easily, and possibly move past a block you have been feeling. Cutting the energetic cords of past relationships or situations allows you to move forward into your future without carrying a past that no longer serves your highest good.

This tool was a life changer for me.

Next I will share a guided meditation with you. It's a very simple meditation and once you have done it, it will be easily repeated to remove any unneeded energetic ties. This can be done as often as you feel necessary. I recommend once a month for a while, until you feel you've released unwanted energy that's been tying you to the past. Then listen to it once every few months for good measure.

It is recommended to also cut cords with people you are still currently engaged with, so that new cords may begin to grow. This will help you to remove old stagnant energy, making room for new fresh energy.

What are energetic cords? Each person or situation we encounter in our lives creates an invisible energetic cord. Sometimes they are thin and long like a thread, such as someone you meet at the grocery store. Other times they are dark, thick and short as in an intimate relationship. The cord attaches your Heart Chakra to the other person's Heart Chakra. This guided meditation will help you to visualize this and give you the opportunity to cut and release the person or situation at the other end of the cord.

You may want to dim the lights and light some candles. If you have crystals, you can include them as well. Perfect additions for this meditation are Clear Quartz for Archangel Michael, Green Aventurine for Archangel Raphael and Rose Quartz for Archangel Chamuel. They are part of your Heart Activation Toolkit. Selenite can also help with cleansing the space.
(See the link for Mending Hearts Crystal Therapy in QR code)

CORD CUTTING GUIDED MEDITATION

At this time, you will listen to the Cord Cutting Guided Meditation.
Create a beautiful and quiet space for yourself if you are able at this time, or schedule a time very soon for your meditation. Be sure to have uninterrupted time to do this. This is the third of eight guided meditations custom written and recorded with a live Sound Bath just for this program.
This Guided Meditation is intended to assist in Cutting energetic cords to relationships or situations that no longer serve your highest good. Specially channeled by me just for you.

Cord Cutting
Guided Meditation

Assignment

Record your experience on the following journal pages. Feel free to share in the Heart Activation Facebook group if you feel called. (Link to join private group in QR code on page 13.)

If you are struggling with this, please reach out through the contact form in the QR link. You are not alone in this process. I will do all I can to support you. You may need a one-on-one session at this point.

Integration-Week Distance Card Reading

During Integration Week, I recommend a distance card reading to help you understand where you are on your journey. This intuitive session connects with your Spirit Guides and Guardian Angels to receive meaningful guidance and insight. While not required, this practice is a powerful way to receive support and clarity as you move through the program.

I conduct these readings remotely using Tarot and Oracle cards and layouts specifically designed for this course. Energy knows no limits, so a distance reading is just as effective as in person. I begin by calling in your energy along with your spiritual support team—Spirit Guides, Guardian Angels, Ancestors, and Ascended Masters—with the intention of receiving messages grounded in Love and light.

Your reading will be video and audio recorded, with clear pictures of your cards and the intuitive messages I receive. You'll receive everything within 48 hours. Each reading throughout the program is $40. To book, use the QR code provided below. It reserves space on my calendar, but the reading itself is done privately. If you'd rather connect live, choose the $60 option for a one-on-one session, either in-person or virtual.

Integration-Week
Distance Card
Reading

Module 2
Perspective

"Change the way you look
at things, and the things
you look at change."
— Wayne Dyer

When you shift your perspective,
your experience of reality shifts
too—even if nothing outside of
you changes.

Module 2: Perspective
Lesson 4: Breaking Through Obstacles

Often after surviving emotional or mental trauma (which often comes along with physical trauma) and living with complex PTSD (c-PTSD), people can come to a place in their healing journey where they feel stuck, unable to move forward and also unable to go backward. They are unsure of what to do. This can be considered an emotional brick wall.

It felt that way to me. I knew I had so much potential, but I couldn't break free of the feeling of futility and pain, both emotional and physical.

Ganesh, the Obstacle Breaker, was introduced to me by one of my coaches to help me break through that emotional wall. A prominent Hindu god, Ganesh is known as the remover of obstacles and the god of wisdom, intellect, and new beginnings. He is easily recognizable with his portly human body and elephant head. In Hindu mythology, Ganesh is believed to bring good fortune, prosperity, and success to his devotees.

You can call on Ganesh with an obstacle breaker chant. An obstacle breaker chant is used like an affirmation, repeated over and over. It might help you remove obstacles that may be keeping you from moving forward in your life. (More on Affirmations in Module 3 Lesson 7 Part 3.)

There are many versions of this obstacle breaker chant. The one I share in this lesson is my favorite so far.

Listening to and repeating the following obstacle breaker chant helped me to break past my emotional brick wall. How or why did it work? I don't know. I can only say that it is energetic. The shift in my energy—or frequency—allowed me to move past what held me back.

This obstacle breaker chant might help you break through your own emotional brick wall. This chant is in the Indian language: *Om Gam Ganapat aye Namaha*. This means:

Om: Name of Creation
Gam: Secret power and sound of Ganesha's name
Ganapat aye: Another name for Ganesh the Obstacle Breaker
Namaha: I see your holiness, and I thank you

You will listen to it and repeat this chant 108 times, a sacred number that can be significant in manifesting the desired effects. Why 108 times?

1 symbolizes everything
0 symbolizes nothing
8 symbolizes infinity

I find this chant to be very soothing, and I have come to enjoy it.

If you find the words of this chant feels like worshiping idols, write your own affirmation with a similar meaning to the chant. For example:

I choose now to remove any obstacle from my energy and matrix.
I never allow other people to create obstacles for me.
I am the only person able to create obstacles for myself, and I choose to stop this practice.
I choose to remove all obstacles that no longer serve my highest good.
And so it is.

The recording of this chant can be found in the link on the next page.

Obstacle Breaker Chant

If you need help counting to 108 while you chant, you could use mala beads. Simply touch or move one bead at a time as you repeat the chant to keep track of how many times you've said it.

Assignment

Repeat this obstacle breaker chant 108 times each day for one week.

Record your experience on the following journal pages. Feel free to share in the Heart Activation Facebook group if you feel called. (Link to join private group in QR code on page 13.)

How did the obstacle breaker chant make you feel?

Did you have any breakthrough moments?

Module 2: Perspective
Lesson 5: Gaining Understanding
Part 1: Storytelling

In this lesson, we are going to discuss perspective. We spend our lives surrounded by other people who experience situations with us. More often than not, we are experiencing these situations through different lenses.

Shifting our perspective and remembering that we are all spiritual beings here on Earth having a human experience can help us to see that everyone's perspective is their personal reality. Respecting this will give you more peace on your journey, knowing you don't need to be right or wrong.

Experiments have been done that help us understand this. For example: Ten people were brought into a room, then another person walked through the room. When each of the ten people were asked what they saw, they each gave a different memory of the person they saw. Everyone focuses on different parts of a person or situation. So, what was the reality? Each person was right. No one was wrong.

Another example is the Necker Cube Test: Enhancing Communication and Collaboration, which found: Understanding the diversity of human perception is also essential for effective communication and collaboration. By acknowledging that other people might have different perspectives and interpretations of the same information, we can work toward finding common ground and developing shared understanding.

We all have our own perspective. We all have stories we tell. We repeat stories to other people about specific situations we have lived through, especially those that are memorable or traumatic. These stories become threads in the fabric of our lives. Often other people who experienced those situations with us will recall them with different perspectives. Many arguments with loved ones begin this way. Two people see the same situation differently, causing conflict.

But can we hold the possibility that both people are right? Can we have compassion for another person that they believe what they are saying is correct? How do we know what the reality is? (Clearly there are situations where another party is not telling the truth. Be aware of the difference between a red flag and a disagreement on perspective.)

Our reality is actually our perspective. Holding onto the stories that we tend to repeat tethers us to our past. Releasing these stories, having compassion and forgiveness for other people, and letting go of the trauma will allow you to move forward more easily.

Assignment

On the next journal pages, write three stories that you tend to repeat. Consider writing about a traumatic situation that has stuck with you. (We will do more with this during Module 2 Lesson 6: The Full Moon Release Ceremony.)

Once you have written these stories, reevaluate them, and do your best to rewrite them having compassion for the other person's perspective.

Do you see how perspective can change?

Record your experience on the following journal pages. Feel free to share in the Heart Activation Facebook group if you feel called. (Link to join private group in QR code on page 13.)

Module 2: Perspective
Lesson 5: Gaining Understanding
Part 2: Understanding Karma

From Wikipedia:

Karma (/ˈkɑːrmə/, from Sanskrit: कर्म{, IPA: [ˈkɐrmɐ] ⓘ; Pali: kamma) is an ancient Indian concept that refers to an action, work, or deed and its effect or consequences. In Indian religions, the term more specifically refers to a principle of cause and effect, often descriptively called the principle of karma, wherein individuals' intent and actions (cause) influence their future (effect): Good intent and good deeds contribute to good karma and happier rebirths, while bad intent and bad deeds contribute to bad karma and bad rebirths. In some scriptures, however, there is no link between rebirth and karma. Karma is often misunderstood as fate, destiny, or predetermination.

Karma is a commonly used phrase these days: Karma's a bitch! Karma's gonna get ya! But is Karma really our enemy? Is it out to get us?

Not at all. Karma is really just the philosophy that what we do comes back to us. So yes, perhaps if someone does bad things, bad things will come to them. But Karma can be your friend as well because if you do good things, good will come to you. How we live our lives and what energy we put out determines our Karma because what we put out comes back to us. That's why it's important to treat people how you want to be treated, even if the person you are showing kindness to isn't very kind back. That's their Karma, not yours.

The idea of Karma connects with the Golden Rule:
"Do unto others as you would have done unto you."

Karma also connects with the Law of Attraction, which is one of the 12 Universal Laws. The Law of Attraction means that you can create the life you want through your thoughts and attitude. Most humans don't understand that we are all powerful creators. We can use our minds to create what we want to see around us. (More on this in Module 4 Lesson 11 Part 1.)

One of my favorite things to do is to be nice to grumpy people! A few years back on a church marquee, I saw the saying, "Be nice to your enemies. It will confuse them."

Holding on to anger and resentment is like giving yourself poison and hoping it will kill your enemy. It's only harmful to you. On the other hand, forgiving other people and having compassion for them will allow you a peaceful life, knowing you are doing the right thing by yourself and karma!

It is said that unresolved Karma can be carried with us through many lifetimes. In our past lives, which could number in the millions, we have done things that brought Karma. We might have died in a lifetime before we were able to resolve a particular situation, so we might still carry that Karma. That might be why you struggle with certain challenges over and over in this life. These are called Karmic cycles.

For example, you might struggle to hold a relationship. You might choose the wrong partners over and over. You might be unable to release unwanted weight—and nothing works to release it. Or you might have chronic pain or an ailment that you can't resolve, no matter how many practitioners you see. Past-life regression hypnosis can possibly help you find out what happened and show you why you might be replaying a situation over and over.

Learning about Karma can help you move forward. Having that awareness, identifying patterns, and taking the opportunity to change them might help you learn the lesson you need to learn to break free of that Karmic cycle.

It is said that women carry generations of Karma. In other words, in addition to our own Karma from past lives, we also might carry our mother's Karma, and her mother's, and her mother's, etc.

We are born with ovaries and carry all the eggs we will ever have with us. So did our mother, and when she was in her mother's womb, she picked up her mother and grandmother's Karma, and so on and so on, and we now carry all of that as well.

How might you identify that you have generational Karma? Have you ever lived through lessons that didn't resonate with you, leaving you wondering *Why is this happening to me? Why can't I learn this lesson already and move on?* If you feel stuck and unable to understand, you might be dealing with generational Karma.

You can break this cycle by expressing:

"I am voiding this contract and releasing any energy that no longer serves my highest good!"

Repeat as many times as you feel necessary and be sure to say it with true intent! Mean it!

Voiding any contracts created by your Ancestors (during their human experience, or even before they came to Earth) might free you to grow in your own journey without the heavy weight of old Karmic agreements that were made before you were even thought of! If you are unable to free this Karma, it might be Karma accrued in your past lives. For that I recommend working with a past-life hypnosis regression therapist or someone trained in Quantum Healing Hypnosis Therapy (QHHT), which is a technique developed and perfected by Delores Cannon. She has many books available dictating her sessions with people delving into past lives. I listed one of her books in the Recommended Reading List which, you can access with the QR code below.

Below I recommend a Certified Master Hypnotist who has trained under renowned Hypnotists. Her information is in the link below, along with other recommended practitioners.

Recommended
Practitioners

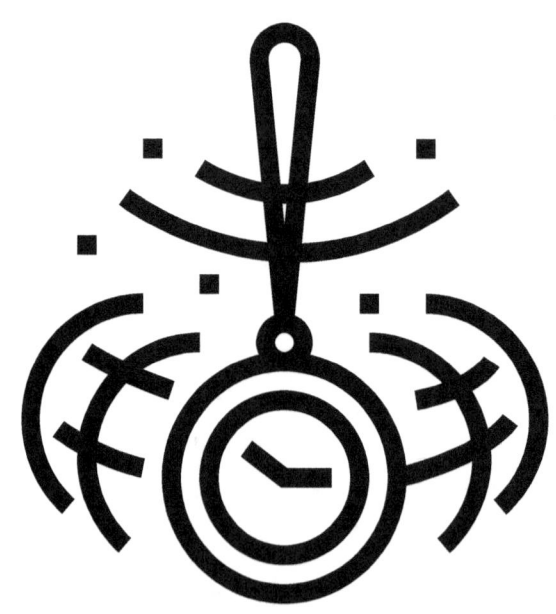

Module 2: Perspective
Lesson 5: Gaining Understanding
Part 3: Understanding Dharma

From Wikipedia:

Dharma: Key concept in Indian philosophy and Eastern religions, with multiple meanings. Dharma is a key concept with multiple meanings in the Indian religions, among others. Although no single-word translation exists for dharma in English, the term is commonly understood as referring to behaviors that are in harmony with the "order and custom" that sustain life, "virtue," or "religious and moral duties."

In **Hinduism**, dharma denotes behaviors that are considered to be in accord with Ṛta—the "order and custom" that makes life and the universe possible. This includes duties, rights, laws, conduct, virtues, and "right way of living." The concept is believed to have a transtemporal validity and is one of the four Puruṣārthas.

In **Buddhism**, dharma refers to "cosmic law and order," as expressed by the teachings of the Buddha. In Buddhist philosophy, dhamma/dharma is also the term for "phenomena."

In **Jainism**, dharma refers to the teachings of Tirthankara and the body of doctrine pertaining to the purification and moral transformation of humans.

I explain Dharma as our payment to the Universe for the lessons we will receive while we are here on Earth. For instance, my creating this program would be considered Dharma. I took what the Universe has taught me, and I am sharing it with you.

This doesn't mean you should write a book or create a coaching program. It might mean that you help a friend or even a stranger. It could mean paying for the coffee order of the person behind you in line. The ripple effect that could cause might change the trajectory of the whole universe! Never underestimate the power of kindness.

I share this philosophy with you to help you understand your purpose here. As we live and learn in this lifetime, I believe it is our duty to pay it forward. No matter where we are on the journey of life, people are following in our footsteps. We are never the only ones dealing with particular issues.

Being vulnerable and sharing with others helps them not to feel alone, and it is also an opportunity to pay our Dharma to the universe.

I consider vulnerability to be a superpower. Because I was a shy, backward child, it is important for me to be open and share what I learn.

Bringing this all together, storytelling, Karma, and Dharma bring us the opportunity to understand our purpose in this life. They allow us to understand the energy of our human existence, and they teach us right from wrong. They help us to shift our perspective about people who have hurt us, understand that what we put out comes back to us, be grateful for what we have been taught through our difficult lessons, and encourage us pay it forward by helping the people behind us on the path.

Assignment

Is there a pattern that you seem to keep repeating?

What lesson might you need to learn from that pattern?

What are you doing to "pay it forward?"

Record your experience on the following journal pages. Feel free to share in the Heart Activation Facebook group if you feel called. (Link to join private group in QR code on page 13.)

Module 2: Perspective
Lesson 5: Gaining Understanding
Part 4: Writing Your Book of Life

Think of your life as a novel. You are the main character, and there are many other characters—maybe a hero, a villain, and a love interest. You can break your novel up into chapters, sections, paragraphs, and even sentences.

In addition to being the main character, you are also the author. You decide who comes and who goes in your story. Some characters will last through the whole book, others will only be in one chapter, and still others will last only a sentence or two.

But all too often, we hold onto a "character" who no longer belongs in our story. You might feel obligated to keep them, or you might still love them, but they might not be what's best for you any longer. They've served their purpose, but you hold onto them past their expiration dates.

If someone does not fit your story any longer, let them go! Thank them for the good memories and lessons they brought you, then send them off with Love. Release them so they might begin their next chapter as well!

Also like a good book, your story has drama, cliff hangers, and celebrations. Wouldn't your story be boring without excitement, mystery, and suspense? On the other hand, there can be too much of a good thing, and going through life being completely traumatized at pitfall after pitfall, speed bump after speed bump would be exhausting. The lesson here is that like a good book, your story will have both good and bad times. This understanding helps us to remember that when things are bad, they will be good again sometime. And vice versa.

Learning that gave me peace during difficult times in my life.

No matter your age, your book still has blank pages. Fill them as you see fit!

Assignment

Reflect upon this concept:

Are there characters in your book past their expiration date who you should let go?

Listen to "Unwritten" by Natasha Bedingfield

Record your experience on the following journal pages. Feel free to share in the Heart Activation Facebook group if you feel called. (Link to join private group in QR code on page 13.)

"Unwritten"
Natasha Bedingfield

Module 2: Perspective
Lesson 6: Full Moon Release Ceremony

Be sure to plan this lesson the week of a Full Moon. Even better, it's ideal to do this exactly on the Full Moon. If you cannot do it exactly on the Full Moon, do it the day before or within three days after.

A Full Moon Release Ceremony is a powerful tool to support you in releasing past people or past energy that is no longer for your best and highest good. It's also time to manifest what you desire. It's a beautiful way to give yourself some Self-Love. In this Full Moon Release Ceremony, we will use the power and energy of the Full Moon to release and manifest.

Understanding the moon cycle can help us better understand our own energetic cycles. I don't believe we are designed to live in a linear pattern. Instead, we are designed to honor and respect the cycles of the moon, and also the Earth, the Sun, and the Seasons.

The moon cycle is a 28-day period that begins with the New Moon and ends with the Full Moon. As we all know, the Seasons are a cycle too: Spring is a time for birth and new. Summer is a time for growth. Fall is a time for harvesting what you have grown. Winter is a time for rest and reset, preparing for the next Spring to come.

In my collaborative book *Wise Woman: Maiden, Mother, Crone*, I delved deeper into these cycles and how they work.

Houses of Light Stories
Wise Woman: Maiden, Mother, Crone
The Seasons of Our Lives
Tami Jean

Did you know the Moon is important in astrology?

Many of us understand our astrological Sun sign. That's where the Sun was in your natal (birth) chart. Your natal chart is an astrological chart of where all the planets were on your chart at the moment of your birth, including which sign they were in (such as Aries, Taurus, or Leo) and in which house.

But the Sun is not the only factor that determines who we are. It is also relevant where the other planets are in your natal (birth) chart, in particular for this lesson, the Moon.

In astrology, the Moon represents emotions, so you can better understand your emotions by learning where the Moon is on your natal chart.

For example: If your Moon is in Aries, you could be like a ram and prefer to power through difficult emotional times, possibly ignoring your feelings or pushing them down when they should be expressed. If your Moon is in Leo, you could be very fiery when it comes to expressing your emotions, maybe blowing up before stepping back and evaluating a situation. (We'll delve into this more in Natal Chart Module 3 Lesson 8.) In the following pages, you will be directed where to get your natal chart read.

Here's how to prepare for your Full Moon Ceremony:

First, gather your Full Moon Release Ceremony tools. Here is a list of suggested items to have during your ceremony.

- Crystals, specifically White Moonstone, plus any others you are called to use
- Candles
- Lighter
- Notebook
- Pen
- Metal bowl, fire pit, or fireplace
- Incense
- Flowers

- Oracle cards (I recommend Moonology by Yasmin Boland or any Oracle deck you have or feel drawn to.)
- White sage bundle
- Pala santo stick

Here is a list of *suggested* items to have after ceremony.

- A bath with essential oils and Himalayan Sea salt
- Essential oil blend to diffuse during the five-day Full Moon cycle (two days before to three days after the Full Moon) for cleaning and clearing:
  - 3 drops eucalyptus essential oil
  - 2 drops thyme essential oil
  - 2 drops lemon essential oil
  - 2 drops tea tree essential oil

To prepare for the Full Moon Release Ceremony, identify a sacred space. Set up your space by placing the crystals around you and lighting the candles. Open the space by saying something like, "I am opening this space for my Full Moon Release Ceremony."

Cleanse the space by burning the white sage bundle for removing negative or residual energy and the Pala santo stick to bring in positive Love and light energy.

Call in your Spirit Guides, Angels, Ancestors, and Ascended Masters, then pull one to three Oracle cards to find the energy that's important for you to focus on during this particular ceremony.

Take three sheets of notepaper or tear one sheet in thirds. Then write a letter to each person you wish to release. It could be short, such as:

"Dear Joe, I forgive and release you as I move forward into my new, healthy energy."

Or you can even just write their name.

Then say this Full Moon Release Prayer or write your own:

I call in all of my Guides and Angels, Ancestors, and Ascended Masters.
Bless this space and affirm my intentions to release all that no longer serves my highest good.
I release all people, situations, and energy that are not for my best interest.
I release all fear, insecurity, doubts, and obstacles and allow in only love, light, and people who have my best interest at heart.
And so it is.

After you have finished your prayer, you can safely burn (or tear up into tiny pieces) the letter(s) you have written. Set the pieces or ashes aside to bury outside later.

Close your space by expressing gratitude for the experience and for being able to release old, unneeded energy. While in prayer hands express any of the following

Namaste' (Indian)
Aho (Native American)
Thank you (English)

After your ceremony, spend time in the bath you have created, or at least sit in the ceremony space and focus on what you have released. Visualize releasing the person or situation, seeing them float away into smoke or dust. Allow them to leave. Focus on the things you are grateful for, such as the people who care for you and accept you as you are, whether they be friends, family, or even colleagues.

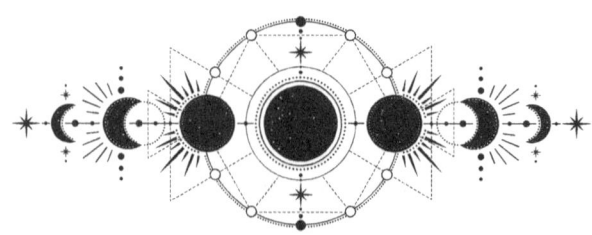

Full Moon Release Guided Meditation

At this time, listen to the Full Moon Release Guided Meditation. This guided meditation is intended to assist in releasing old energy and clearing room for the new, which you will manifest in the next module.

Create a beautiful, quiet space for yourself. Be sure to have 60 uninterrupted minutes to do this.

This is the fourth of eight guided meditations I wrote and recorded with a live Sound Bath for this program.

Record your experience on the following journal pages and feel free to share your experience in the Heart Activation Facebook group if you feel called to.

Full Moon
Release Guided
Meditation

Record your experience with the Full Moon Release Ceremony on the following journal pages.
Feel free to share in the Heart Activation Facebook group if you feel called. (Link to join private group in QR code on page 13.)
Plan your Natal Chart Reading (see next page) and your Integration-Week Card Reading (see page 85).

Natal Chart Reading

An important tool in this program is a Natal Chart Reading. We will discuss the details and relevance of this reading in Module 3 Lesson 8.

Use the link below to share your information so a personalized Natal Chart Reading can be created for you. Simply provide your birth date, time, and city through the form. With this information, your chart will be prepared and the most important themes will be highlighted to support you in understanding your unique journey. Each reading is $40.

Within about two weeks, you'll receive your chart image along with a clear explanation of the key insights and guidance revealed—offering you a deeper look into the area's most meaningful for your path.

*This reading may be done by me or an associate of mine. No personal information will EVER be shared. Your privacy is VERY important to me.

Natal Chart
Reading Form

Integration-Week Distance Card Reading

During Integration Week, I recommend a distance card reading to help you understand where you are on your journey. This intuitive session connects with your Spirit Guides and Guardian Angels to receive meaningful guidance and insight. While not required, this practice is a powerful way to receive support and clarity as you move through the program.

I conduct these readings remotely using Tarot and Oracle cards and layouts specifically designed for this course. Energy knows no limits, so a distance reading is just as effective as in person. I begin by calling in your energy along with your spiritual support team—Spirit Guides, Guardian Angels, Ancestors, and Ascended Masters—with the intention of receiving messages grounded in Love and light.

Your reading will be video and audio recorded, with clear pictures of your cards and the intuitive messages I receive. You'll receive everything within 48 hours. Each reading throughout the program is $40. To book, use the QR code provided below. It reserves space on my calendar, but the reading itself is done privately. If you'd rather connect live, choose the $60 option for a one-on-one session, either in-person or virtual.

Integration-Week
Card Reading

Module 3
Understanding

"The wound is the place
where the light
enters you."
— Rumi

True understanding often comes
through pain. It opens the heart
and deepens perception.

Module 3: Understanding
Lesson 7: Manifesting
Part 1: New Moon Manifestation Ceremony

Using the power of the Moon, you can create the life you desire and deserve through intention setting and by doing a New Moon Manifestation Ceremony.

New Moon energy is a time to set your intentions of what you would like to manifest in your life. What are intentions? They are our desires and dreams that we want to turn into reality. A new relationship, career, or home are common things people would like to see happen in their lives.

We can create phrases to repeat inwardly or out loud to ourselves about what we desire. These phrases are sometimes called "mantras." Repeating these mantras can help us to release old, stagnant energy and allow new energy into our matrix. The trick is to believe what you are saying. Say it as if it is already in existence. (More about intention setting and creating affirmations in the next section.) I recommend reading through this lesson and the Affirmation and Intention Setting (Module 3 Lesson 7 Part 3) lesson before performing your New Moon Manifestation Ceremony.

You can create your own intention statement or here are some suggestions:

- I release what no longer serves me and welcome new opportunities into my life.
- I am open to receiving and allowing the Love I deserve and desire from myself and others.
- I let go of fear and embrace change, growth, and transformation.
- I am in alignment with my highest purpose and manifest my dreams.
- I am grateful for the abundance that flows into my life.

As with the Full Moon Release Ceremony, create a sacred and beautiful space.

First, gather your tools. Here is a list of suggested items to have during your ceremony.

- Crystals, specifically Black Moonstone, plus any others you are called to use
- Candles and Lighter
- Prepared intention statement
- Incense
- Flowers
- Oracle cards, optional (I like *Moonology* by Yasmin Boland.)
- White sage bundle
- Pala santo sticks

For after the ceremony and during the New Moon cycle:

- Prepare a bath with essential oils, Himalayan Sea salt, and candles
- Suggested essential oil blend to diffuse during the five days of the New Moon cycle (two days before the New Moon and three days after) for cleaning and clearing:
  - 2 drops clary sage
  - 2 drops sandalwood
  - 1 drops lemon
  - 1 drops frankincense

Preparing for the ceremony:

Set up your space, including placing the crystals around you. Light the candles. Open your space by saying, "I am opening this space for my New Moon Manifestation Ceremony."

Cleanse the space by burning the white sage to remove negative or residual energy, the Pala Santo stick to bring in positive Love and light energy. Call in your Guides, Angels, and Ancestors. Draw a card or cards to find the energy that's important for you to focus on during this ceremony. This will be helpful if you aren't sure what you want to focus on.

Then say this New Moon Manifestation Prayer.

I release what no longer serves me and welcome new opportunities into my life/matrix/space. (Choose which word resonates with you.)
I am open to receiving and allowing the love I deserve and desire from myself and others.
I let go of fear and embrace change, growth, and transformation.
I am in alignment with my highest purpose, and I manifest my dreams.
I am grateful for the abundance that flows into my life.
And so it is.

Clearly state your intention with feeling. Repeat it up to five times if you feel called to do so.

Close your space by expressing gratitude for the experience and for being able to manifest what will be for your highest good. Allow the new energy to enter your matrix.

While in prayer hands express any of the following

Namaste' (Indian)
Aho (Native American) or
Thank you (English)

Spend time in a bath or the sacred space you have created for a while after. Visualize what you have intended. Feel what you want as if it already is. For example, close your eyes and see that perfect-for-you romantic partner, the beautiful office you desire, or the quaint A-frame log cabin you've always dreamt of!

Feel it in your core, as if it is all around you. Feel how good it feels, as if it is happening right now. Never underestimate your power to manifest the life you deserve!

New Moon Manifestation Guided Meditation

At this time, you will listen to the New Moon Manifestation Guided Meditation.

Create a beautiful and quiet space for yourself if you are able at this time or schedule a time very soon for your meditation. Be sure to have uninterrupted time to do this. This is the fifth of eight guided meditations I wrote and recorded with a live Sound Bath just for this program.

This Guided Meditation is intended to assist in manifesting new energy and can be used when you are attempting to create anything new. Specially channeled by me just for you.

New Moon
Manifestation
Guided Meditation

Record your experience on the following journal pages.

Feel free to share in the Heart Activation Facebook group if you feel called. (Link to join private group in QR code on page 13.)

Module 3: Understanding
Lesson 7: Manifesting
Part 2: Using Frequencies

Several years back during a very painful flare-up of diverticulitis, I added frequencies to my toolkit. At that time, I learned several healing tools, including juice cleansing and sound baths, attempting to heal my body without taking antibiotics because they negatively affect my digestive system.

I believe antibiotics are a miracle. However, in my opinion, they are over-prescribed without the additional advice to support your digestive system with pre- and probiotics to keep your gut biome healthy.

I was in a desperate fight to avoid antibiotics, and I did so for two weeks. But at the advice of a holistic nurse practitioner I was introduced to through a local health food store, I finally took them. Even though by then I was feeling mostly better, she felt it was safest for me to take them so that I could completely clear the infection. She assured me that she would assist me in rebuilding my gut health afterward. I had just spent several years recently fighting a candida yeast overgrowth, and I did NOT want to go back there. However, I did not want to have half of my colon surgically removed either, which was another option presented to me by a conventional medical doctor. That was a common solution for untreated diverticulitis, and it was not a risk I was willing to take.

I fought a good fight using natural remedies, and I came out of it with a lot of knowledge about the digestive system and what actually causes diverticulosis, which can lead to diverticulitis. After this experience, I am now also on a path to become a Holistic Herbal Practitioner, or Medicine Woman, as I prefer to be called. It was important for me to understand more to be able to help others when the opportunity arose.

At this point, I was led to sound baths and one of my future coaches through very strange and interesting circumstances. A gentleman knocked on my apartment door selling energy services—from an electric company provider, not energy healing. Somehow, we got on the subject of my health issues and my use of natural remedies. He suggested I meet his friend and boss who is a sound-bath healer.

When I met the sound-bath healer, he briefly explained frequencies to me. Frequency is the number of waves that pass a point in one second. They are measured in Hertz, Hz. The most important thing to remember is that everything is energy. And all energy carries a frequency. Humans generally vibrate between 60 and 70 Hz.

The sound-bath healer also explained frequencies' ability to help heal physical and emotional issues. After doing some research, I learned that a 432 Hz frequency helps with healing in general. I added that tool to my arsenal and so began another branch of my journey.

Here are suggested frequencies to help you create the life you desire:

- 396 Hz: Transform guilt into forgiveness
- 417 Hz: Facilitate change
- 432 Hz: Foster grounding/connecting to Mother Earth
- 528 Hz: Stimulate love
- 639 Hz: Heal relationships

Lower frequencies also have a purpose, particularly in keeping us grounded. We can utilize these frequencies to assist us in grounding meditations. Many people avoid lower frequencies because they are trying to raise their vibration while they ascend into becoming higher vibrational beings, but it's important to maintain proper balance. As with anything, each level of vibration has value.

How can we use frequencies?

There are many ways to do this. One option is to find a local wellness center or yoga studio that has live sound-bath healing. We have a beautiful salt cave near us, and the owner has a sound healer come in monthly to play her crystal bowls, among her many other tools. We are able to lie in the salt, which is very grounding and healing within itself, as we allow the frequencies to wash over us and heal our bodies at a mitochondrial level. All of the guided meditations included in this program have been created by a talented sound healer and me specifically for you!

You can also find sound baths for many different purposes on YouTube.

Here's a list of several frequencies and what they are helpful for. I like to play these when I'm working on jewelry, for background music in the house, or when I'm resting. Frequencies work even while you sleep!

- For resting, I prefer a whole-body healing frequency, such as 174 Hz or 528 Hz used for cell regeneration. (Page 103)
- For grounding, I love a shamanic drumming frequency 328 Hz, which supports balancing Root Chakra issues such as fear and releasing negative patterns.
- When I am working with the Archangels, such as during the Cord Cutting Meditation, I prefer a high frequency, such as 852 Hz.
- Working with healing the Heart, physically and energetically through the Heart Chakra, you can use 528 Hz and 629 Hz.

Physical is all energy as well. As we discussed in the first lesson, you can shift your frequency by expressing gratitude and by holding a more positive attitude. This frequency will attract similar frequencies.

On the other hand, if you exist in a low vibrational frequency, you will attract other low-frequency beings.

Here are some simple things you can do if you feel lower vibrationally to raise your frequency.

- Rose water naturally vibrates at 320 Hz. Mist into your face, about 12 inches away, and breathe deeply.
- Carry or wear as jewelry high-vibrational crystals, such as amethyst (200-400 Hz) and clear quartz (32,768 Hz).
- Use essential oils, which each have unique frequencies. Suggestions:

Idaho blue spruce 580 Hz	Chamomile 105 Hz
Rose 320 Hz	Myrrh 105 Hz
Helichrysum 181 Hz	Melissa 102 Hz
Sacred frankincense 147 Hz	Juniper 98 Hz
Ravintsara 134 Hz	Hawaiian sandalwood 96 Hz
Lavender 118 Hz	Angelica 85 Hz
Blue tansy 105 Hz	Peppermint 78 Hz

As I mentioned, people naturally vibrate between 60 and 70 Hz. If you do these things to raise your natural vibration, you are not going to go up to 528 Hz instantly. That would kill you, or maybe you would disappear into another dimension! Not really sure about that! What it will do is raise your natural vibration to a level your body can handle. And the more you work with frequencies, the higher the frequencies your body will be able to handle. Your natural frequency will constantly shift, depending on the energy around you and your feelings. For example, if you're feeling depressed, your frequency will be in a lower state. When you're having a great day, your frequency will naturally be higher.

As you work with frequencies, your natural state will remain higher for longer periods, though it's important to understand that it will always shift up or down. This is part of life. However, as you reach higher consciousness (or Christ Consciousness), your frequency will tend to stay higher. Over the last few years, there has been a lot of information coming through psychics and channelers helping us to understand that as humans we are evolving into a higher frequency state of being. This is a big subject. I recommend looking into channelers such as Lee Harris and the Z's, Darryl Anka and Bashar, or Abraham-Hicks to learn more about this. There are many videos on YouTube or their websites.

Assignment

Listen to the Full Body Cell Regeneration Frequency recording below. Sit back, close your eyes, and let the sound of the frequency wash over you.

Record your experience on the following journal pages. Feel free to share in the Heart Activation Facebook group if you feel called. (Link to join private group in QR code on page 13.)

Feel free to search around for a frequency recording that feels good to you or fits your current need.

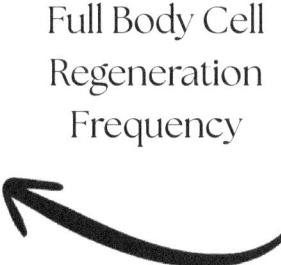

Full Body Cell
Regeneration
Frequency

Module 3: Understanding
Lesson 7: Manifesting
Part 3: Intention Setting and Affirmations

Intention setting is clearly, consciously choosing what you want to create, feel, experience, or shift—emotionally, physically, mentally, or spiritually. An intention is more than just a goal; it's an energetic declaration of what you're ready to embody or invite in.

Intentions are like seeds planted in your energy field. They begin to shift your focus, change your frequency, and open pathways for healing. When you pair intention with holistic practices, you amplify their impact.

The best way to manifest your intention is by creating affirmations. This is how you plant those seeds to begin to create permanent change. An affirmation is a few words or a sentence declaring what you want to see in your world. Often, they are repeated, over and over, or several times an hour, day, week, month, etc.

When I first learned about affirmations, I thought they were useless. I felt silly saying the same thing repeatedly. I was also in a place where I hated my voice.

But a few years ago while I was working with a coach, she explained that affirmations were part of her program. I expressed my dislike of them, so of course, she pushed me on it! She knew their power. I am very glad she pushed me because they changed my life!

By repeating a statement, you are putting it out into the Universe. You are declaring to the Universe what you would like to see. What you put out will come back in time.

According to Abraham-Hicks, we are putting it in our "Vortex," as with the 17-Second Rule. We are putting it into our energetic field, which will in turn, attract like energy. As with the Law of Gravity, the Law of Attraction is very real! What you put out you will get in return.

Here's how to set intentions and then write affirmations. First list up to 10 things you would like to see different in your matrix. These are your intentions.
Example: "I want to be an artist and create beautiful art that many people want to buy."

1._____
2._____
3._____
4._____
5._____
6._____
7._____
8._____
9._____
10._____

Now choose your top five. Adjust them to make them current, actually true today, to turn that dream into a reality. These are your affirmations.
Example: "I AM *an artist who creates beautiful art that many people are buying* NOW!

1._____
2._____
3._____
4._____
5._____
6._____
7._____
8._____
9._____
10._____

When you are ready, create affirmations from all 10 of your intentions. Remember, you can use these tools in any way you would like! Feel free to play with them.

Now that you have created your affirmation, say each of them 10 times a day for one week. You can say them out loud, or in your head. It does not matter, as long as you say them with conviction! You can alternate them, or you can say them sequentially. It doesn't really matter. You can memorize them, but you do not have to.

However, the more often you say your affirmations, the more they will stick! You will find yourself saying them as you do dishes or fold laundry. This can be a form of meditation as well.

After one week, repeat them each 25 times a day for another week.

After the second week, repeat them each 40 times a day for another week.

I actually recorded myself saying each of my affirmations 50 times, and I listened to that recording over and over. It was a bit difficult for me to remember them all, so if this is an issue for you as well, you can try this method. I played 432 Hz frequency music in the background as I recorded myself saying them. (432Hz is for grounding and bringing energy into reality.)

That worked for me! Do what works for you!

Assignment

Record your experiences with repeating affirmations and if you see any changes taking place. Be sure to say your affirmations with conviction!

Feel free to share in the Heart Activation Facebook group if you feel called. (Link to join private group in QR code on page 13.)

Module 3: Understanding
Lesson 8: Natal Chart Review

A natal chart is an astrological chart of where the planets were on your chart at the moment of your birth, including which sign they were in and in which house. If you're brand new to astrology, I'll explain more.

Most of us know our birth zodiac sign. There are 12 zodiac signs, including Aries, Taurus, and Libra. For example, if you were born on July 27, you are a Leo. This is also called your "Sun sign." It indicated in which zodiac sign the Sun was at the time of your birth. Your Sun sign gives an overall description of who you might be, but there is a lot more to astrology!

In addition to the Sun, there are 10 influential planetary bodies in astrology, including Jupiter, Saturn, and the Moon. The day you were born, each of those planets was in a "house" or piece of the pie chart and a zodiac sign.

For example, if you were born on July 27, 1970, your Sun sign is Leo, your Moon sign is Taurus, your Mercury sign is Leo, and your Venus sign is Virgo. Each of the planets affects a different part of your personality. The Moon influences your emotions. Virgo informs your relationships. And Mercury is about communication, which is why when Mercury is in retrograde (seeming to move backward in the planetary cycle), our communication devices and skills seem to fly out the window.

To give you an idea, if you were born under Virgo Sun with your Moon in Libra, it might mean you're very organized and also balanced emotionally when it comes to love relationships. You might also be very balanced and precise in decision making. If Mercury is in your sixth house (career) when you were born, you could end up a public speaker. You are definitely not afraid of speaking in front of a crowd.

As far as I'm concerned, astrology is a whole different language! It's a lot to learn and understand. I have some basic knowledge of it, enough to know how important it can be in our daily decision making.

Having your natal chart done might offer insight into why you are the way you are and why you do the things you do.

Learning about my natal chart helped me to understand why I was divorced twice and enabled me to forgive myself. Apparently, I wear rose-colored glasses when I meet people. Now I know to watch for red flags, and I know not to ignore them! Apparently, it's difficult to see red flags through rose-colored glasses! Who knew?! I also learned that when I meet someone, I don't have to accept their flaws and fix them! I need to take care of myself and make better choices when it comes to my own well-being.

Knowing your natal chart can also empower you with the opportunity to change things that you would like to see differently. Perhaps you want to quit a bad habit or stop a weird behavior.

Having the information from your natal chart can give you a plethora of insight that might help you to better understand yourself, accept your imperfections, and love yourself unconditionally!

Assignment

By now you should have received information back from me about your natal chart.

Use the following journal pages to record your thoughts and feelings about your natal chart reading and any ah-ha moments.

Feel free to share in the Heart Activation Facebook group if you feel called. (Link to join private group in QR code on page 13.)

Module 3: Understanding
Lesson 9: Forgiveness
Part 1: Forgiving Yourself

On my healing journey, I wanted to forgive people who hurt me, intentionally and unintentionally. Many people have trauma from those they love and who love them because of thoughtless, hurtful things that have been said or done. Some people were raised by verbally abusive, disrespectful parents who didn't truly care about them or what was in their best interest. Unfortunately, many parents have expectations of their children, and if we don't meet those expectations, they are consistently disappointed in us. This can be quite damaging.

A few years ago during an Ayahuasca ceremony, I set intentions to find forgiveness and compassion for people who hurt me. I learned that I held so much resentment toward myself for my mistakes that there was no way I could forgive anyone else. I couldn't find forgiveness and compassion for others if I didn't have it for myself. This was a big eye-opener for me.

If you can go within and find compassion and forgiveness for yourself for your mistakes or bad decisions, you will then be able to find that for others. I go deeper into this in a book I co-authored called *Houses of Light Stories: Going Beyond the Programming-Falling in Love with Myself.*

Houses of Light Stories:
Going Beyond the
Programing of Your Life
—Falling in Love with Myself

Here's a technique that might help you forgive yourself. What if those things you think were mistakes and bad decisions were actually lessons to build you into the person you are now. For example, if I hadn't made my many "bad decisions," I would not have acquired the knowledge I'm sharing with you in this book. My "bad decisions" brought me to a place where I feel confident enough to share what I've learned to hopefully help other people who are on a similar journey as mine.

Assignment

Use the journal pages to write the mistakes you have made and how you can find compassion for yourself.

Feel free to share in the Heart Activation Facebook group if you feel called. (Link to join private group in QR code on page 13.)

Module 3: Understanding
Lesson 9: Forgiveness
Part 2: Our Personal Power

Because of our cultural mindset programming, you have likely given away your power so that you could fit in, make other people happy, or keep the peace with an abusive partner or family member, which is generally futile. It's time to take back your power!

Why should you take back your power?

To truly reclaim your power, you must first take responsibility for your own actions. I remember watching an episode of Dr. Phil when he said something that struck me deeply: "People only treat you the way you allow them to treat you."
That moment shifted something in me. Blaming others for everything that's happened in your life may feel justified, but it also hands over your power. It keeps you stuck in the role of the victim.

When you begin to take ownership of your part—even in the hardest experiences—you begin to heal. You stop giving others control over your peace, and in doing so, you grow stronger, more self-aware, and more empowered than ever before.

**"No one can make you feel inferior without your consent."
—Eleanor Roosevelt**

Forgiveness is a key factor in this. This can be a very difficult area for most. How can you forgive someone who has hurt you?

This was definitely challenging for me. I was very angry with my abuser to the point that it was poisoning me and keeping me from moving forward in my life. And believe me, I had good reason to be angry. I tell this story in my chapter in *Houses of Light Stories: It's Time to Honor the Light Being Within—The Wounded Healer.*

I'll give you the short version here. (See the link for the book in the QR code on page 121.)

I have spent a lot of time teaching other people that "everyone is your teacher," but that had not sunk in for me in this situation. One day as I was driving, it hit me! He was my teacher. It all made sense! That was his role in my life, and because of him, I learned all these tools that I teach you now. Suddenly all of the anger, resentment, and hurt I felt toward him washed away. Believe me when I say, this was no small miracle!

Less than two weeks later, I learned he had a terminal illness. In that moment, with the same deep inner knowing, I understood that his purpose in this lifetime had been fulfilled. Within a year, he was gone.

For years, I struggled to forgive him—and always came up short. It wasn't until I began to extend compassion and forgiveness to myself that I realized: I couldn't offer those things to anyone else until I first gave them to myself. That was one of the most profound lessons of my life.

When you hold anger for someone who has hurt you, who does it hurt? It hurts you. As I mentioned before, it is like taking poison and hoping your enemy will die. It's exhausting and fruitless. Until you forgive that person, you give them your power. You continue to be the victim. Forgiving that person and having compassion that they are on their own journey will give you your power back, allow you to move on with your life, and bring you the peace you have been searching for.

Assignment

On the following journal pages, write some of your hurts and how you can forgive and find compassion for those who have hurt you. Feel free to share in the Heart Activation Facebook group if you feel called to.

Module 3: Understanding
Lesson 9: Forgiveness
Part 3: Finding Authenticity

Being truly authentic to yourself and others is not always easy. This was difficult for me because I didn't understand what it meant until I was close to 40 years old. I remember when I was fairly young, my mother telling me to "just be yourself." I couldn't even wrap my head around that. I could easily morph myself into anything I wanted, or more likely into what someone else expected of me.

At some point, I learned that when I got comfortable around people and I began to let down my guard, they didn't seem to like me anymore. Later I realized that I wasn't showing people my true self from the beginning. Instead, I was showing them who I thought or perceived they wanted me to be. Once they saw the true me, I wasn't really their cup of tea. Which is fine! The key is that if you are yourself from the get-go, people who don't like people like you will steer clear, and people who do like people like you will come forward.

Instead of doing the things other people enjoy, find the things you would like to do. In turn, you will find other people who like the things you like! What a concept!

Assignment

What hobbies do you enjoy, or what is something you would like to try?

Where are some places you would like to visit?

Feel free to share in the Heart Activation Facebook group if you feel called to. (Link to join private group in QR code on page 13.)

Integration-Week Distance Card Reading

During Integration Week, I recommend a distance card reading to help you understand where you are on your journey. This intuitive session connects with your Spirit Guides and Guardian Angels to receive meaningful guidance and insight. While not required, this practice is a powerful way to receive support and clarity as you move through the program.

I conduct these readings remotely using Tarot and Oracle cards and layouts specifically designed for this course. Energy knows no limits, so a distance reading is just as effective as in person. I begin by calling in your energy along with your spiritual support team—Spirit Guides, Guardian Angels, Ancestors, and Ascended Masters—with the intention of receiving messages grounded in Love and light.

Your reading will be video and audio recorded, with clear pictures of your cards and the intuitive messages I receive. You'll receive everything within 48 hours. Each reading throughout the program is $40. To book, use the QR code provided below. It reserves space on my calendar, but the reading itself is done privately. If you'd rather connect live, choose the $60 option for a one-on-one session, either in-person or virtual.

Integration-Week
Distance Card
Reading

Module 4
Love

"Where there is love,
there is life."
— Mahatma Gandhi

Love is not just an emotion.
It is the animating force
behind all creation.

Module 4: Love
Lesson 10: Returning to Wholeness
Part 1: Connecting with Your Inner Child

What is the inner child?

The inner child is a part of each of us. As we become adults, we still carry the young child version of ourselves, among all of the different ages and versions of ourselves.

I learned of this while working with a trauma therapist after my second failed marriage. She helped me understand all of the different parts we carry with us, what they feel like, and what each of them has to do with the whole.

Specifically, the inner child is what we feel when we need love, affection, and comfort. If you are not receiving these basic human needs from your family or loved ones, your inner child will begin to express herself to let you know she is feeling neglected. When we don't feel loved or that we are not getting the attention we need, the feelings bubble up in the form of loneliness, self-pity, or desperation—especially when it comes to finding a lover.

As a young teenager after moving with my father and my grandparents across the country from my mother, I became desperate for love and physical affection. As a child, I often felt I was a burden. I was told to be quiet or to go to my room. When I offered an opinion, I was shushed. That's why I did not have the confidence to be myself and speak my truth, until much later in life. Because I was not getting the attention I needed, I began to search out attention from the opposite sex.

Throughout my life, I showed signs of sexual abuse, but I had no memory of that. While reading *Queen's Code* by Allison Armstrong (the sequel to *Keys to the Kingdom*, which I referred to in Module 4 Lesson 12), it hit me full force. It wasn't sexual abuse in the way we would normally think. It was me being allowed to spend time alone with young men and become sexually active long before I was mentally or emotionally prepared. This left a scar and became a way I got the love I so desperately needed. I felt I needed to have sex to receive love, and I did not understand it was the other way around. No one had taken the time to explain the emotions behind sex or how to respect myself. Because of this, I struggled for many years with relationships and marriage until I was in my late forties. Both of Allison Armstrong's books completely shifted my understanding of marriage and relationships.

As most parents do, mine did their best. They taught me what they were taught. This is where generational programming comes into play. We can break this cycle. I believe I did with my sons because I taught them to speak up so they weren't afraid of their voices, like I was. They are definitely not afraid to speak up!

During my trauma therapy, I learned to recognize when my inner child was in need. I began to use journaling, which was highly recommended by my therapist, and I allowed my inner child to speak through my writing.

There are two ways to use writing to work with your inner child. First, you can ask your inner child what she has to say, then write whatever comes. Or you can write a letter to your inner child, giving her comfort or saying whatever you feel needs to be said.

Later, I worked with a hypnosis therapist, who guided me to visit my five-year-old self. I was able to spend time with her, play with her, and give her the comfort she needed and might not have received during that time period. It was a beautiful opportunity to tell her she is okay and that I love her very much.

As an only child, I played alone a lot. I don't mind being alone, even today, but it was important that as an adult I sat on the floor with my inner child and played. She needed that attention. I often find myself doing that now with children I encounter. Parents often get busy with life and forget to play. I wish I had played with my boys more, and I plan to play with my grandkids whenever I get the chance!

Another way to connect with your inner child is through meditation. There might be a particular situation you went through at a specific age. You can go within and connect with that version of yourself, during that difficult time. You can go in as the current version of yourself, with the lessons you have learned and help comfort the younger version of yourself. (More on meditation in Module 5 Lesson 15 Part 3.)

Playtime

As adults, we often forget to take time to play. We get so caught up in being adults that we forget to have fun. Monotonous routines of everyday life take over, and we mindlessly go through each day, forgetting to pay attention and to stop and smell the roses. Playing can ease your inner child's needs.

Here are playful things you can do. Look back on your childhood. What did you enjoy doing? Do that!

- Riding a bicycle
- Coloring
- Gardening or planting flowers
- Creating a fairy or gnome garden
- Climbing a tree
- Playing and building sandcastles at the beach
- Running around with your kids, grandkids, or dog
- Playing with building blocks
- Building a model car
- Doing diamond art
- Painting
- Building a birdhouse
- Birdwatching
- Dancing like nobody's watching

- Blasting your favorite music and singing like nobody's listening

I could go on, but you get the picture. Lighten up and enjoy the things you may have when you were a child.

"Stop taking life so damn seriously!" —My Angel Guides

Assignment

Take time to play. Use the following journal pages to record your playtime activities.

Color the image below and on pages 149-153 and don't be afraid to color outside the lines!

Do the Connecting to your Inner Child Guided Meditation on page 148 and record your experiences on the journal pages.

Feel free to share your experiences and the pictures of your art in the Facebook group if you feel called to.

Connecting to Your Inner Child Guided Meditation

At this time, you will listen to the Inner Child Guided Meditation.

Create a beautiful and quiet space for yourself if you are able at this time or schedule a time very soon for your meditation. Be sure to have uninterrupted time to do this. This is the sixth of eight guided meditations I wrote and recorded with a live sound bath just for this program.

This guided meditation is intended to assist in connecting with your inner child at any age that might be needed. It is an opportunity to play with her and connect in a way that you can give her comfort and support she might not have received. Specially channeled by me just for you.

Inner Child
Guided
Meditation

153

Module 4: Love
Lesson 10: Returning to Wholeness
Part 2: Falling in Love with Yourself

One of the most important lessons I learned was how to fall in love with myself. Think of how you would like to be treated by a lover or someone you are interested in romantically. Now apply that to yourself. List on the journal pages what you would like to receive from a romantic interest, or how you would like to be treated. Would you like to be spoken to kindly and sweetly? Would you want to be touched in a tender way? Would you like to hear how beautiful you are and how they can't stop looking at you? We are all different, of course, so write down what you would want. Then do it for yourself. If you would expect it from someone else, then expect it from yourself! No one can love you like you can! Know your worth and know that the person you have been searching for is within you.

Creating this energy will begin to attract that energy from others. If you do not allow the Love from yourself, you will never truly allow anyone else to love you in the way you deserve. If you feel you don't deserve love, you won't attract it. This is all about the frequency you are emitting. (Review the lesson on frequencies in Module 3 Lesson 7 Part 2.)

Here are some ways to show yourself Love.

- Buy yourself flowers.
- Drink a glass (or bottle) of your favorite wine.
- Make yourself your favorite dinner.
- Buy yourself dinner from your favorite restaurant.
- Go for a walk in the local park or rose garden.
- Sit by the ocean on a pretty blanket with a picnic.
- Read a book and drink tea under a cozy blanket.
- Watch your favorite movie.
- Take a bubble bath with wine, flowers, essential oils, and candles.
- Pleasure yourself.

"You Are Who You've
Been Looking For!"
by Adam Roa

Assignment

Listen to "You Are Who You've Been Looking For." (Above link)

List three things you have done for yourself and how they made you feel. Use the list of suggestions on page 154 or come up with your own.

Feel free to share in the Heart Activation Facebook group if you feel called to.

Module 4: Love
Lesson 11: Shifting Reality
Part 1: Creating Your Matrix

I love the term "matrix" to describe our reality, our space. The space around us is what we have created. Understanding that humans are very creative beings helps us to understand why our reality looks like it does.

We have been created by a great Creator. There are many names we use for this energy, such as God, Sophia, the Divine, Source, Allah, Yahweh, and the Almighty. Humans tend to need to label things and put them into neat little boxes. I believe this subject is much bigger than we could ever comprehend with our limited intelligence.

Many of us feel stuck where we are in our family, career, or community. Yet we grew up here and struggle to see anything different.

Similar to how I believe we chose to join the family we seemingly landed in, I also believe we chose who we surround ourselves with as we mature physically and spiritually. But we also have the power to change them!

Your parents were chosen before this life, and there is a good reason for that. But as you grow and expand into your own authenticity, sometimes it's okay to shed the people you got stuck with here on Earth. There are innumerable circumstances. I'm here to say that it's okay to remove yourself from unpleasant situations. You do not need to tolerate crazy Aunt Martha or creepy cousin George any longer!

The situation you might want to shed could be a career that doesn't bring you joy or a loveless marriage. You have made many choices in your life, and I believe that you made them for good reason. You had lessons to learn. It's time to take the lesson, release the undesirable energy, and create a life you can love!

The frequency you currently hold is attracting what you see. If you do the work and raise your vibration, balance your Chakras (aura or energetic field), and open your Heart space, you can attract beautiful energy into your matrix.

As I shifted my energy and evolved as a human, I was able to almost completely change my surroundings. (Check out my chapter in the *Houses of Light Stories: It's About Time to Honor the Light Being Within —The Wounded Healer*. Link in QR code.) I created stronger, closer relationships with my sons, I found a man who treats me like a queen, and I have become accepted as a part of his family and been "allowed" to make his house OUR home. Through my transformation, I learned about activating my Heart, which is where this program stems from. I learned to allow others to love me and truly be able to receive the love they are sending. I have surrounded myself with amazing friends and created a business I love. I have become better at removing people around me who do not serve my highest good. If someone does not feel good to be around, I distance myself from them. I choose not to be brought down by other people's stagnant, negative energy.

Am I perfect? Absolutely not! Far from it! Sometimes I need to read my own articles to remind me who I am! I have friends I can go to who help lift me up and remind me who I am. Because I am a mother effin' unicorn and a queen, and I deserve what I see around me! Some days I struggle. But every day has gotten better. I'm not sure c-PTSD ever goes away, but I certainly have many more good days now than bad ones! And you can too!

Red Pill

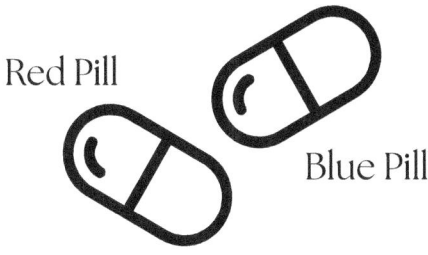

Blue Pill

Assignment

Notice your surroundings. How do they feel? Do they bring you joy? Or do they make you want to run away and live on an island somewhere?

How do the people in your life make you feel? Are you able to be yourself around them? Or do you have to be fake to keep them around? Does someone give you the creeps, but you aren't sure why?

Trust your gut (intuition) on this! Maybe they aren't an awful human, but there's something about them that just rubs you the wrong way. Trust that feeling. You are not wrong! Being aware of these feelings, otherwise called that "still, small voice" will assist you in realizing who is vibrating in your frequency and who is not.

Once you raise your frequency, people and situations might fall away! It can be quite magical! Sometimes it will hurt, and that's okay.

I recently lost a friend who I felt was a soul sister. At first, I blamed myself, but in time, I realized that I was healing, and my frequency increased. She no longer matched my frequency. Once I became aware of this, I was able to have compassion for her situation and need to separate from me, and I was able to forgive myself for believing that this was my fault. I thanked her energetically for the love and lessons she had brought into my life, and I let her go.

Awareness is key in many of these situations. The more you can step back and see the bigger picture, the less you will take things to heart. Take the lesson learned, feel the emotional pain, then release it.

Record your feelings on the following journal pages.

Feel free to share in the Heart Activation Facebook group if you feel called to.

Module 4: Love
Lesson 11: Shifting Reality
Part 2: Boundary Setting

In our American culture, we have been programmed to put our feelings aside for the sake of others. We tolerate people and their behavior, so it doesn't upset them or others.

Finding, accepting, and loving yourself might require you to set new boundaries, especially around family members who think they know you or have certain expectations for you.

However, you will definitely run into people who will not respect your boundaries. When this happens, it might be important for you to reiterate how important this is to you. If they truly love you and want what's best for you, they will respect you. And if they do not, you do not want them in your matrix. And I don't care who it is. It's time to leave them in the dust! And it doesn't matter how it makes anyone else feel. It matters how it makes you feel!

As in Module 2 Lesson 5, we learned about storytelling and your book of life. This is your book, and you are the author! No one else!

Assignment

When was there a time that you wished you could have set a boundary and didn't?

Using the journal pages that follow write a brief story around that situation and what it could look like if you would have set that boundary, and why you didn't.

If you can't think of an idea, on the next page are some prompts to help you get started.

Feel free to share your experience in the Heart Activation Facebook group if you feel called to.

- Jumping when someone calls for help
- Saying yes every time you get an invitation
- Agreeing with people to avoid arguments or disappointment
- Doing things to avoid hurting others feelings
- Putting others before yourself
- Appeasing others so they like you

Module 4: Love
Lesson 11: Shifting Reality
Part 3: Understanding Heart Activation

As mentioned in the Heart Activation opening statement, I discovered this concept during my two failed long-term relationships. One of the key points in this circumstance is that we were all well into our forties. As people age, we might have had several unsuccessful relationships, so we could possibly become jaded and/or closed off to love. Having been hurt too many times, it becomes difficult for some people to be open to love. Love becomes a difficult concept with painful memories attached to it, so we avoid it, and we don't truly let people in.

With this program, my intention is to help you shift your perspective to understand the true meaning of love and to activate your Heart. By healing past trauma, shifting your perception of your reality, and understanding that love comes from within yourself, you can find forgiveness and compassion for yourself—and then for other people.

Finding that forgiveness allows your Heart to activate. For some people, this might be a reactivation, while for others it might be the first time.

As babies all we knew was love, the love of our Creator and hopefully our parents. Some of our damage might have come from well-meaning parents or from a partner or partners who did not have our best interest at heart. This might be why it's time for you to find that love within yourself.

This all came to a head for me after my second failed long-term relationship when I realized I wasn't allowing my father to love me. We had always had a strained relationship. My knee-jerk reaction when he offered to help me was always to say no. I understand now I was punishing him for what he had "done to me." As a teenager, desperate for the affection from my father, I made very bad choices. As an adult, I blamed him for my difficulties in life because he didn't love me the way I thought he should. At the time, he was raising a teenage daughter alone, and looking back, I think he thought it was inappropriate to hug me and say I love you.

When I was 48 years old, after my second Ayahuasca ceremony, I came home early, completely defeated and emotionally drained. My father did not know where I had been. I had told him I was going to a yoga retreat because he wouldn't have understood what I was doing. When I came home early, he could see something was wrong and was concerned for me. He offered to make me some food, and I instinctively said no. As I sat there, I realized what I had done. He offered to nourish me, and I did not allow him to do so. It dawned on me that it was his way of showing love, and I quickly changed my answer and accepted his gift. (Refer to *The 5 Love Languages* by Gary Chapman.) I realized that I had not allowed my father to show me love in the way he knew how and that might have caused a lot of our relationship difficulties.

Once we allow, or accept, a gift being offered to us, it is important for us to receive it with gratitude of heart. It's important to express gratitude, but also to really feel it. This is an important energy shift. Otherwise, we can accept a gift without being grateful.

Think of a time when you gave a gift and it was accepted, but not received gratefully. How did that make you feel?
On the other hand, how wonderful does it feel when you give a gift and the person receiving it lights up in gratitude? We can allow someone to do something kind for us, but can we truly receive the gift with gratitude?
An important part of Heart Activation is expanding your Heart to allow other people to love you and being able to receive their Love with gratitude.

In my relationship with my father, I did not see the gift he was offering me. Learning about the love languages helped me to see he was doing the best he knew how. I was able to find compassion for him and receive his gift with gratitude.

Assignment

Use the QR code below to assist you in expanding your Heart center. This song is a 24-minute mantra intended to shift the energy around your Heart and allow it to expand to feel Love and compassion for yourself and also to let other people in. Sit or lie in a meditation position and let the words wash over you, allowing it in. Visualize your heart space as a green ball of light and feel the words and music penetrate your body.

Share your experience on the following journal pages and in the Facebook group if you feel called to.

Expand from
Heart Center Mantra
Aad Guray Namay
-Jai Jagdeesh

Module 4: Love
Lesson 12: Sacred Sovereignty
Part 1: Seeking Interdependence

Relationships can be a very expansive subject. We quite literally have relationships with everyone we come into contact with—everyone from our favorite nail technician and our massage therapist, to the guy who details our antique muscle car. (Bear with me, I'm manifesting here). We have relationships that last from childhood to relationships with our newest bestie! Parents, siblings, and family members are all relationships, as are friends, coworkers, partners, and lovers. We can't forget our furry friends! Those are generally the best—creatures that get excited when we arrive home, even if just from getting the mail, who cannot contain their excitement! Unless you have a cat...but I digress.

The main relationships I want to discuss here are our life partners, lovers, and spouses. These can get very complicated. And they are the relationships most likely to throw you off course from finding that most important Love—with yourself.

All too often, we put ourselves last in our Love relationship. You might have been taught that putting yourself first is selfish. Our American society pushes women to follow steps to get to a certain place in life. We are programmed to believe we should go to school, college, build a career, get married, have a family, and retire to quilting or golf.

We often put our dreams aside to do "the right thing." We sacrifice to raise our families for what? To one day find that we don't even know who we are, married to someone we barely know anymore, with no clue what we want in life. In this part, I want to talk about two pitfalls of relationships—extreme independence and dependency—and then the goal of interdependency.

Independence, being a strong person who can stand on your own two feet, can be a beautiful thing.

For the purpose of this lesson, I want to discuss the unhealthy type of independence—the extreme type of independence where a person has decided she doesn't need anyone. She might have chosen to be alone because she was hurt too many times. She might have chosen to close her Heart to the possibility of Love because it's too painful.

If this sounds like you, recognize this was a choice you made. And so it is a choice you can unmake.

Codependency can be described as being too dependent on another person and unable to rely on your own opinion or intuition, or unable to trust yourself.
Codependency can be caused by a narcissistic partner who creates a situation where you don't trust yourself, through degradation or gaslighting, making you feel like you're crazy. Codependency can also be caused by a lack of self-confidence, fear of abandonment, or trauma from childhood or past relationships. It can also be subconscious, possibly from past-life traumas or unpaid Karma from this or a past life. It can also be an unhealthy situation to the partner of a codependent person. It can be very smothering to the partner.

We might not understand where extreme independence or codependence stems from, so therapy or coaching can be helpful. Being able to create a safe environment with someone you trust who is professionally trained is a good place to start. The key starting place is awareness, which is what I intend to bring to you in this book. Being aware of what is happening is the first step in finding your way to an *interdependent* relationship. Interdependency is the goal of a relationship. It's the state where you and your partner are both dependent on each other—to a healthy extent.

Interdependency occurs when two people function as whole beings, able to work together, support, and encourage each other without fear or jealousy. Once you are whole and love yourself, you will be able to find a partner who is whole and loves themself as well. You will both be able to trust each other and the love you have for each other.

Interdependency is a beautiful place to be.

The state of interdependence can be reached when you and your partner are both capable of trusting yourselves and your intuition and when you both are whole people in love with yourselves.

But on the other hand, once you truly understand and love yourself, you might come to a situation where you find yourself content and peaceful, happy just living in your own skin—not looking for or needing a partner at all.

Module 4: Love
Lesson 12: Sacred Sovereignty
Part 2: Looking for Red Flags

When we go into new relationships, we often see only the best in our new love interest. If we do sense some flaws, we overlook or ignore them. We are high on love. Many people want to see the best in someone or something—especially in the beginning.

However, especially later in life, many people become more skeptical in new relationships. Because we have been through some difficult times, it is important to focus on the lessons we have brought with us on our journey and leave the emotional pain behind.

My intention with this section is not to scare you away from new relationships, but to bring you awareness as you enter into them. Being aware of red flags can assist you in better decision making and being able to determine the difference between a flaw, a cute little quirk, or a red flag. Then you can decide whether or not to continue the relationship.

Here are red flags to look for when entering a new relationship of any kind.

- Narcissistic, self-focused behavior
- Controlling behavior
- Too-good-to-be-true behavior
- Degrading comments
- Questioning your opinion or ideas constantly, making you question yourself.
- Making you feel badly about yourself
- Commenting negatively about others to build their ego
- Talking AT you not TO you
- Not listening when you speak
- Speaking over you and making you feel your opinion has no value
- Yelling or losing their temper easily
- Having double standards

If you are with someone and you see any of these signs and your gut is nudging you that something isn't right, feel into that. Trust your intuition and find the courage to do what is right for you and your future. If possible, try to see the situation from an outside perspective. What would you advise someone else, like your sister or best friend, to do in this situation? Now treat yourself with the same respect and grace.

Assignment

Read or listen to the following recommended reading suggestions in your own time. I prefer audiobooks so I can get other things done while listening.

Use the following journal pages to record your thoughts and feelings about these books. Feel free to share in the Heart Activation Facebook group if you feel called to.

Keys to the Kingdom by Allison Armstrong
The 5 Love Languages by Gary Chapman

Integration-Week Distance Card Reading

During Integration Week, I recommend a distance card reading to help you understand where you are on your journey. This intuitive session connects with your Spirit Guides and Guardian Angels to receive meaningful guidance and insight. While not required, this practice is a powerful way to receive support and clarity as you move through the program.

I conduct these readings remotely using Tarot and Oracle cards and layouts specifically designed for this course. Energy knows no limits, so a distance reading is just as effective as in person. I begin by calling in your energy along with your spiritual support team—Spirit Guides, Guardian Angels, Ancestors, and Ascended Masters—with the intention of receiving messages grounded in love and light.

Your reading will be video, and voice recorded, with clear pictures of your cards and the intuitive messages I receive. You'll receive everything within 48 hours. Each reading throughout the program is $40. To book, use the QR code provide below. It reserves space on my calendar, but the reading itself is done privately. If you'd rather connect live, choose the $60 option for a one-on-one session, either in-person or virtual.

Integration-Week Distance Card Reading

Module 5
Integration

"When you touch one thing
with deep awareness,
you touch everything."
— Thich Nhat Hanh

True integration means living fully
present in the moment—where
body, mind, and soul align.

Module 5: Integration
Lesson 13: Caring for Your Body
Part 1: Physical Self-Care

Taking care of your body is very important in this journey. You have come into this body as an Eternal Soul, and keeping your body healthy is crucial to being able to experience what you came here to do. Now, obviously there are situations where one's journey will include a physical disability, injury, or illness, which might have been beyond one's control. That might actually be an important part of the lesson you are here to learn.

However, that does not mean that you aren't to take the best care of the body you were given and show gratitude for what you have. (Module 1 Lesson 1: Gratitude). Being here on this Earth plane is a great blessing and shows that prior to this life, you made a very important choice to be here. You did not have to do this. So kudos to all of us for just being here!

Treating your body as a vehicle, giving it the proper care, movement, and fluids it requires, will provide you the opportunity to keep that vehicle as long as possible. As you would your car, it is important to get proper maintenance, keep everything lubricated with high quality oils, and fill your tank full of the best fuel, or at least the best fuel for your particular vehicle. If our bodies do not get the proper maintenance and use the proper oils and fuels, they will degrade and eventually break down.

Each of our bodies is similar, but very different at the same time. For example, according to Ayurveda, your body type might require a particular fuel. They believe food is medicine, and your body type and constitution will determine the best foods for you to use as medicine. Although there are many cultures and ways of eating, I have found that following Ayurvedic principles is the best alternative for my body.

Ayurveda is an ancient holistic healing system from India that focuses on balancing the body, mind, and spirit through natural methods. It's based on the idea that each person has a unique combination of three energies or "doshas"—Vata (air and space), Pitta (fire and water), and Kapha (earth and water) —and that health comes from keeping these doshas in harmony. Ayurveda uses diet, herbal remedies, lifestyle practices, and self-awareness to promote wellness and prevent disease.

It can be very beneficial to work with a holistic nutritionist to learn your body's specific needs. In the following QR code you will find Recommended Practitioners. I highly recommend connecting with my suggested practitioner or one in your area to find the best fuel for your body.

Americans are offered poor food choices in most grocery stores. The USDA Food Guide Pyramid even recommends a grain-heavy, low-fat diet—an approach I believe contributes to widespread illness. Add in preservatives, harmful oils, such as vegetable and corn oil, pesticides, and dyes, and it's no wonder the food on our shelves is making us sick.

Recommended Practitioners and Reading List

Assignment

Connect with the recommended nutritionist or someone local to you.

On the following journal pages, list your food intake for the next seven days. This will be beneficial when connecting with a nutritionist.

Food Journal

Day 1:

Breakfast: _____
_____

Lunch: _____
_____

Dinner: _____
_____

Snacks:_____
_____

Water Intake: _____

Day 2:

Breakfast: _____
_____

Lunch: _____
_____

Dinner: _____
_____

Snacks:_____
_____

Water Intake: _____

Day 3:

Breakfast: _____
_____

Lunch: _____
_____

Dinner: _____
_____

Snacks:_____
_____

Water Intake: _____

Food Journal

Day 4:

Breakfast: _____
_____

Lunch: _____
_____

Dinner: _____
_____

Snacks:_____
_____

Water Intake: _____

Day 5:

Breakfast: _____
_____

Lunch: _____
_____

Dinner: _____
_____

Snacks:_____
_____

Water Intake: _____

Day 6:

Breakfast: _____
_____

Lunch: _____
_____

Dinner: _____
_____

Snacks:_____
_____

Water Intake: _____

Food Journal

Day 7:

Breakfast: _____

_____

Lunch: _____

_____

Dinner: _____

_____

Snacks:_____

_____

Water Intake: _____

Module 5: Integration
Lesson 13: Caring for Your Body
Part 2: Sleep Routine

Just as we created a morning routine in Module 1 Lesson 1, here we will create a sleep routine to ensure proper rest. Here are some ideas to consider.

- Be sure to set boundaries with your family that this is your time. Make this a sacred part of your day.
- Create a sleep space that is sacred to you. Your bedroom should be a sanctuary for sleep. Leave problems at the door and allow yourself space to rest and renew.
- I love my silk pillowcase and microfiber body pillow. For me, bedtime is time to build my nest and get super cozy.
- Play nature sounds or a sound bath while sleeping. I advise keeping phones and screens out of the bedroom, but you could put a Bluetooth speaker across your room (not directly next to you) and play whatever sound you love. I love summer night sounds, insects, and thunderstorms with wind chimes. I have also come to love "brown noise" because it is softer and more soothing to me. Rain-Rain is a good app for these sounds because you can combine sounds, and it is very inexpensive to use.
- Keep a journal and pen next to your bed in case you have a dream you want to remember, something you just can't get off your mind, or an amazing thought you don't want to forget!
- Drink one cup of warm water one hour before bedtime. It is said that this will help with brain function.
- Spend at least one hour before bed away from screens to allow your mind to slow down and begin the rest period.
- Sit in bed with a warm light and enjoy a good physical book (not a screen)! This tends to put me to sleep.
- Before falling asleep, express gratitude, release the day, and set intentions for good rest and a fresh start tomorrow.

Sleep is very important for our bodies. Especially for middle-aged, premenopausal women, it is a time in life to begin to slow down. At this time, it's a great idea to take on less responsibility and request more help from your spouse or partner and/or older children. And it's okay to say NO!

Nine hours of sleep is ideal. Creating a less stressful environment in our lives (yes, I hear you grumbling) will lower your cortisol levels, help balance your hormones, and allow you to move into the later stages of life with more ease and grace.

I realize not everyone reading this is middle-aged, so keep this advice in mind as you age or if you are dealing with a mother or grandmother. Try to have compassion for their changing bodies and pick up some responsibilities from them if they will let you!

In our society, mature women tend to take on too much. We were programmed since childhood to put everyone's needs before our own and that self-care is selfish. I'm hoping to help women, like me, to break that cycle.

If you are a younger woman, you can help your older family members break this cycle and teach younger generations a better way to age!

Module 5: Integration
Lesson 13: Caring for Your Body
Part 3: Physical Activity

It is important to note here that exercise is only one part of this equation. We can go to the gym three to five times a week for up to an hour, but what else are we doing? Do we sit or stand in one place at work for eight hours a day?

Creating opportunities to move your body is very important for your physical and even mental health. We need to move to create blood flow, drain lymph, detox the liver, and keep our muscles active. While at work, you can take small steps to add more activity to your day. Purposefully picking things up or stretching while bending for something will create movement. If you need to pick something up, use your knees instead of your back to create a squatting motion. If you are able, get up every half hour or hour to stretch or take a short walk. Even using isotonic movements (flexing and holding muscles) while sitting at a desk or driving can be helpful.

Creating a more active lifestyle can be a solution other than, or in addition to, going to a gym and working out. Here are some ideas to move more.

- Run around outside with your dogs or kids.
- Mow the lawn with a push mower–unless you have 12 acres!
- Wash your car by hand instead of going through a carwash.
- Take the stairs whenever possible.
- Park farther away from a store.
- Move your legs while doing dishes.
- Take a walk.
- Play outdoor games, such as Frisbee, kickball, cornhole, and horseshoes.
- Do winter activities, such as skiing, snowboarding, and snowshoeing.
- Do yoga, tai chi, or Pilates.

- Take a class, such as aerobics, boxing or kickboxing.
- Take a dance class with your partner, such as line dancing or ballroom dancing, or sign up for an adult ballet class.

As noted, exercise is great to remove toxins from your body, but it's not the only way. Here are some other ways to reduce toxins.

- Lymph massage
- Steam room
- Red light therapy

Even if you go to a gym, you might still need to be sure you are moving more often and not just lifting weights. Do stretching and cardio along with strength training.

Assignment

On the following journal pages list which exercises you like to do. If you don't like to exercise, what would you be willing to try? How can you move your body more?

Do you hate exercising? Express why on the following journal pages. What can you do to create movement?

Share your experience in the Facebook group if you feel called to.

Module 5: Integration
Lesson 13: Caring for Your Body
Part 4: Loving Your Body

It is important to love your body. You are given one body to care for during this lifetime. If you aren't happy with your body, the most important step you can take is to love it as it is and have genuine gratitude for the vessel that carries your soul. This can begin to shift your energy through gratitude to create the best body you can have.

In our lesson on Affirmations, we talked about how using affirmations can shift our energy, to begin to attract the life we want. Now, I admit, saying an affirmation about being healthy a thousand times while sitting on the couch eating a bag of potato chips is clearly not going to change your body. However, saying this affirmation might shift the way you think about being healthy. It can drive you to make better choices as to what's going into your mouth, which can give you more energy to want to move your body. This becomes a snowball effect, moving your energy into a more positive direction.

Holding the perspective that we are Eternal Souls having a human experience will help us to appreciate our vessels—despite how they may look. We don't have to have a super-model body to enjoy this human experience.

- Having the understanding that we chose this life experience and this body can help our view on how we feel about our bodies.
- Having an awareness that the diseases and disorders we carry might be part of our journey in this life and appreciating what that may be teaching us. Find the lesson. (Suggestion: Find or start a support group for people with the same disease or disorder as you.)
- Doing our best to fuel our bodies properly and care for our particular disorder to the best of our ability.
- Having gratitude for the challenges because they are here to teach us will also help our perspective of our bodies.

Module 5: Integration
Lesson 13: Caring for Your Body
Part 5: The Value of $100 Bill

Think of this, if someone handed you a $100 bill that was just off the print, what would that bill be worth to you? One hundred dollars, right?

If someone handed you a crinkled, ripped, old, dirty $100 bill, what would it be worth to you? One hundred dollars!

The moral of the story is, it doesn't matter how you look, how you dress, what color your hair is, or if you haven't showered in a week. You are still just as valuable no matter how you look —or smell! Many, many people in the world wear designer clothes and spend hundreds of dollars a week at the salon. They might look and smell good, but that doesn't increase their value as humans, no matter what they might think. Your value as a human shouldn't change, especially to the people who love you.

Assignment

How do you feel about your physical body?

If you aren't happy with it, what steps can you take to change your perspective?

Journal on the following pages and share in the Facebook group if you feel called to.

Module 5: Integration
Lesson 14: Caring for Your Mind

These days, many people deal with anxiety, depression, and other mental disorders. A high percentage of people are on pharmaceuticals to deal with these issues. Of course, I would never suggest to anyone to disregard medical advice. What I do know is that the many tools I discuss in this program helped me wean off of anxiety and depression medications.

Although I won't go too deep into this subject, as I am not a doctor (yet) or a psychologist: In my opinion, too many people are put on unnecessary medications with unfortunate side effects (they're actually just effects) before other methods are tried. I believe this practice is backward. Giving people medication before going to alternate holistic tools just feels wrong to me. Here I will share a few tools that helped me to wean off my medications.

Part 1: Shadow Work

Shadow work is a way to go into those dark places within us that we prefer not to see to discover the gifts within the dark parts, understanding that without dark, there cannot be light, and finding a way to accept and love even those dark parts within us. This is actually a very important part of finding unconditional Self-Love. Unconditional means without conditions. When we hide from these parts of ourselves, we are not truly embracing who we are in all facets.

We might have been programmed in childhood not to show these parts. Many of us were raised with phrases such as "Skeletons in the closet," "Sweep it under the rug," or "Don't air your dirty laundry." However, more and more, through the bravery of people willing to be vulnerable, we are learning that it's okay to have a dark side. It's okay to have flaws, and those flaws are not something to be ashamed of, but something to embrace and love. We are also learning that we are not alone!

Bringing our shadows to the surface can also help us to see the lessons within them. Instead of hiding them, we can acknowledge, love, and release them—if they no longer serve our highest good, retaining the lessons we learned.

Assignment

List some things you might be hiding in the shadows.

What can you learn from them?
What can you accept and release?

Journal on the pages at the end of this lesson and share in the Facebook group if you feel called to.

Part 2: Reiki

Reiki is a gentle, Japanese technique used to reduce stress, promote relaxation, and support healing. It works through light touch—or even no touch at all—and it's based on the idea that a vital "life force energy" flows through all of us. When this energy is low, we're more prone to illness and stress. When it's high, we feel healthier, happier, and more balanced.

The word *Reiki* comes from two Japanese words: *Rei*, meaning "universal wisdom" or "higher power," and *Ki*, meaning "life force energy." Together, Reiki translates to "spiritually guided life force energy."

Although Reiki isn't a religion, it encourages a way of living that supports peace, respect, and harmony with others. Mikao Usui, who founded the modern Reiki practice, shared simple yet profound ethical principles to guide a more mindful and compassionate life—values that resonate across cultures and spiritual paths.

Balancing our energetic field through Reiki can help us to find comfort and peace. Our energetic field (sometimes referred to as our aura) or our Chakras, must spin in a consistent, clockwise fashion. Many times, life, negative energy, poor relationships, or unsatisfying jobs can throw our Chakras out of balance. Having regular weekly or monthly Reiki sessions can help us to stay in balance and have a more peaceful, satisfying, clearer life experience.

Consider finding a local Reiki practitioner near you. (If you live in Eastern Pennsylvania, contact me through the Contact Form provided.) Listen to the Chakra-Balancing Guided Meditation whenever you feel out of balance.

Part 3: Mindfulness

Being present in our lives can help us to feel more centered. Being conscious in the moment can ease anxiety (worry about the future that we cannot control) or depression (regret over the past that we cannot change). We can do most activities with mindfulness, from walking to eating.

Many times, we are lost in thought and are completely unaware of what we just did. Have you ever arrived somewhere and not remembered driving there? Using mindfulness can help keep you present and connected.

Whatever you are doing, be present. Repeat to yourself what you are doing, such as, "I am cutting an onion," "I am walking down the hallway," "I am touching my favorite blanket." Sometimes if I find myself lost in thought, obsessing over something I cannot control, I bring myself back to the present by wiggling my toes or fingers.

Part 4: Grounding (Review)

As discussed in Module 1 Lesson 2 Part 2, grounding can help here as well. Spending 20 minutes daily in the dirt or grass or on a grounding mat if nature isn't readily available will keep your energy grounded, and you will feel less scattered, flighty, or unfocused. There are many tools available to assist in grounding. There are mats you can stand on, sit on, or even put on your mattress for sleep. The best option is nature. However, these other tools are scientifically proven to help as well. Refer back to the Grounding lesson and guided meditation Grounding and Protection in Module 1.

Part 5: The Serenity Prayer

This simple, yet powerful, prayer helped me in so many ways.

God,

Grant me the *Serenity* to accept the things I cannot change,

The *Courage* to change the things I can,

And the *Wisdom* to know the difference.

Amen

Module 5: Integration
Lesson 15: Caring for Your Soul

Humans often find themselves wondering if there's more—something beyond the physical reality we live in. For some, this curiosity is met with what many call a "sixth sense," an inner knowing or intuitive insight about things before they happen. This is how my journey as a lightworker truly began: through these quiet, powerful moments of knowing.

More and more people are awakening to their spiritual gifts. Yet, this awakening can bring challenges, especially when it clashes with deep-rooted beliefs shaped by upbringing, religion, or societal norms. Much of what we've been taught, often passed down through generations, has been programmed into us even before birth, contributing to what we call generational Karma (Module 2 Lesson 5). Realizing that these beliefs are not absolute truths, but fear-based constructs born from the ego, empowers us to break free. When we choose Love over fear, healing begins—and with it, the path forward becomes clear.

Part 1: Trusting Your Intuition

Tuning in spiritually includes listening to your intuition. Our current American life has become busy and chaotic, which has created a breakdown in our spiritual connection.
Have you ever been in a situation where "something" told you to do something, but you didn't listen, then later you thought, "I should've listened." Or have you done the opposite and you listened to that still, small voice, and you did something, despite it not being the right thing to do. Possibly it was a knee-jerk reaction and out of character for you. But it *was* the right thing to do for *you*, despite it being wrong according to what society has taught you.

How do you begin to trust your intuition?

What you perceive as your intuition can be your Spirit Guides,

Guardian Angels, Ancestors, or even your Higher Self. Your Higher Self could also be referred to as your Eternal Soul, your Spirit, or your Subconscious. It is the part of you that is your pure essence—the true YOU, the part that remembers all of your lives, the part that knows you as you truly are, and the part that sees your highest potential (not your limitations). This is the part that knows the lessons you need to reach the next level, and she is here to provide opportunity for growth, expansion, and all the pain and misery that you need to experience to reach that potential. Your Higher Self sees the whole big picture.

Similar to knowing your Inner Child, being aware of your Higher Self can help you see that bigger picture. It can help you to shift your perspective, knowing that everything is in your best interest and will assist in the collective growth in the Universe.

Stepping back and seeing the world as a great big beehive, with many working parts working as ONE great big collaboration, can help to bring us into balance, knowing we are not alone. We are a whole entity connected to Source Light.

You can talk to your Higher Self and ask for support or guidance. Using the Connection to Your Higher Self Guided Meditation (see page 226) will help you see that you are able to connect to that version of yourself anytime you need to. If you have a pertinent question that needs answered, clear your mind, ask the question, stop, and listen. The first thing that comes is your answer. Don't overthink it, don't question it, just listen. In time, this can become a regular practice to support your decision making. You can use this guided meditation as often as you like, or you can just stop, ask, and listen. You will get an answer. But you must have ears to hear.

Ever wonder what's the opposite of your intuition? It's your ego.

Let's discuss our old friend Mr. Ego for a moment. What does ego sound like? It could be your own voice in your head, it could be one of your parent's voices, or it could be someone else's voice such as a former partner. Mr. Ego is tricky. He wants you to be safe! That is his top priority! He will do anything to keep you that way. He is aware of all your past trauma, even things you have forgotten. His job is very important. However, he loves to use scare tactics and manipulation to get you to do what he feels is in your best interest. Mr. Ego never forgets past hurts, and he doesn't want you to forget either.

What Mr. Ego doesn't see are the lessons and growth you have experienced through the pain you have suffered. Having a nice little chat with Mr. Ego might help ease his fear. Let him know you are safe and that you appreciate that he is trying to protect you. Invite him to the table but be sure he is not sitting at the head of it. Express gratitude for all he does to keep you safe but remind him that he is not in charge.

Now the question remains: How can you tell the difference between the voice of your intuition (your Higher Self) and the voice of your ego (your fear)?

Learning to differentiate between the Ego mind and the Intuitive mind might require some practice. Once you understand what they sound like, you will be able to calm the ego and allow the still, small voice of your intuition to shine through. Meditation is a good tool here. Find a quiet space and sit with yourself. Starting with short intervals, allow your mind to quiet. Typically for me the ego sounds like doubt, negativity, and fear. Quiet that voice for as long as you can. This will take practice. Listen into the quiet space and trust that still, small voice when it comes to you. It will feel good. It will feel loving, supportive, and confident. If you feel doubt about what you may have heard, that's Mr. Ego butting his nose where it doesn't belong! Thank him for trying to protect you and ask him to sit down and be quiet.

Part 2: Tuning in Spiritually

As I mentioned previously, part of listening to your intuition is tuning in spiritually. Here are some tools that can help you tune in spiritually.

- Reiki (Module 5 Lesson 14 Part 2)
- Grounding (Module 1 Lesson 2 Part 2)
- Cord cutting (Module 1 Lesson 3)
- Shadow work (Module 5 Lesson 14 Part 1)
- Meditation (see page 224)
- Pranayama or Breathwork (see 224)
- Sound bath healing (see 225)

Each of these tools can help you to tune in to your Higher Self and connect with Source energy, which is called many things depending on your beliefs, such as God, the Divine, Source, Universe, Allah, Yahweh, and Sophia.

Part 3: Meditation

Meditation can be prayer, quieting of the mind, affirmations, or any other repetitive action. Some people find creating art, driving, or doing laundry meditative. Creating art of any type could work for you. Coloring, painting, drawing, building a fairy garden or birdhouse, or gardening is art. Walking mindfully in nature and being present during any activity is meditative. You will find what works best for you. For me, listening to sound bowls or nature sounds, as I'm doing currently, helps me to focus my ADHD energy.

Meditation has always been a struggle for me because it's nearly impossible for me to keep my mind completely clear. I have learned that it is okay for the mind to wander. Also, I do a visualization that helps me with this. If something comes into my mind, I categorize it. If it's something I need to remember, I visualize it being put on a shelf for later. If it's something negative I want to release, I will put it into a trash bag or allow it to dissipate into smoke. If it is something I want to send to my Angels or Guides, I will put it into a bubble to float away, releasing it from my concern. If it is something special that I want to remember, I will put it into a treasure chest for safe keeping.

Part 4: Pranayama

Pranayama, also called breath work, is another great tool you can use to tune in spiritually, mentally, or even physically. It is the art of using your breath to bring focus. Pranayama is used in many practices, such as yoga, sound bathing, forest bathing, simple relaxation, meditation, and grounding.

When going into meditation, I prefer what is called Square Breathing because counting during the breathing helps to keep my mind clear and to have something to focus on. I often use this during my guided meditations, as you might have already heard. This is how it goes.

- Inhale to a count of four.
- Hold your breath for a count of four.
- Exhale for a count of four to six, if you are able. (This helps to release any stagnant energy.)
- Again, hold for a count of four.
- Repeat at least four times, then return to natural breathing.

Part 5: Sound Bath Healing

For a sound bath, you lie on a blanket or yoga mat in a relaxed, meditative posture. You can bring a blanket, pillow, and sleep mask if you choose. The sound bath healer will play many instruments, including sound or crystal bowls, Koshi chimes, rain sticks, and crystal triangles, which each project a unique frequency to bathe your body in healing frequencies. (Module 3 Lesson 7 Part 2.)

Throughout this program you have been experiencing Sound Bath music intuitively played and recorded just for you!

CONNECTING TO YOUR HIGHER SELF GUIDED MEDITATION

At this time, you will listen to the Connecting to Your Higher Self Guided Meditation.

Create a beautiful and quiet space for yourself if you are able at this time or schedule a time very soon for your meditation. Be sure to have uninterrupted time to do this. This is the seventh of eight guided meditations I wrote and recorded with a live sound bath just for this program.

This guided meditation is intended to assist in connecting with your Higher Self. It is an opportunity to go within, sit with your older, wiser self, and ask her for guidance. Specially channeled by me just for you.

Record your experience on the following journal pages and feel free to share your experience in the Heart Activation Facebook group if you feel called to.

Connecting to Your
Higher Self Guided
Meditation

HEART ACTIVATION GUIDED MEDITATION

At this time, you will listen to the Heart Activation Guided Meditation.

Create a beautiful and quiet space for yourself if you are able at this time, or schedule a time very soon for your meditation. Be sure to have uninterrupted time to do this. This is the eighth of eight guided meditations I wrote and recorded with a live sound bath just for this program.

This guided meditation is intended to bring together all of the tools and techniques you have learned in this program and Activate your Heart. Specially channeled by me just for you.

Record your experience on the following journal pages and feel free to share your experience in the Heart Activation Facebook group if you feel called to.

Heart Activation
Guided Meditation

Final Heart Activation Card Reading

Welcome to your final card reading! Congratulations! This reading is designed to give you final advice from Spirit Guides, Guardian Angels, and your Higher Self.

As with all readings in the program, I conduct these readings remotely using Tarot and Oracle cards and layouts specifically designed for this course. Energy knows no limits, so a distance reading is just as effective as in person. I begin by calling in your energy along with your spiritual support team.

Your reading will be video and audio recorded, with clear pictures of your cards and the intuitive messages I receive.

You'll receive everything within 48 hours. To book, use the QR code below. It reserves space on my calendar, but the reading itself is done privately. If you'd rather connect live, choose the $60 option for a one-on-one session, either in-person or virtual.

Share your experiences you may have during this final meditation on the following journal pages, or in the Facebook group if you feel called to.

Final Heart
Activation
Card Reading

Celebration

You did it! I am so proud of you! Take time to celebrate with yourself or someone you love! Do something special for yourself! This is a time to honor your endeavor and steadfastness to become who you have always been, a Warrior!

Once you have completed* the course, fill out the Contact Tami Jean link (using any of the QR codes) to request your Certificate of Completion of the Heart Activation Toolkit Program. I will mail that to you soon after receiving your request.

*Course completion includes purchasing all required readings and recommendations and sharing ALL assignments either privately or in the Heart Activation Facebook group. No exceptions.

Epilogue

As I go through this crazy journey called life, I find that the more I learn, the less I know.

At this point, I am supremely aware that this life is so much more expansive than I believe any human can fathom. Because of the tools I have shared with you, I have come to a place of strength, courage, and humility. Honoring this human experience as I go into the Crone stage of my life, I forgive my younger self for the mistakes made that were not mistakes. I take all of the lessons learned, and I release the fear, insecurity, self-doubt, and disappointment to stay where it belongs, in the past. I choose not to carry it with me into this stage of life.

This is a time for confidence, quiet strength, support of the other women just a few steps behind me on this path, and being an example of what unconditional Self-Love looks like. Because there is always more to learn and there will always be bad days to balance out the good ones, I pray that I will keep my focus on the good and be strong enough to continue to be steadfast in my endeavor.

I am grateful for this opportunity to share my toolkit with you. I sincerely hope that you have grown to a place where you can find love, peace, and hope for the duration of your journey.

In gratitude,

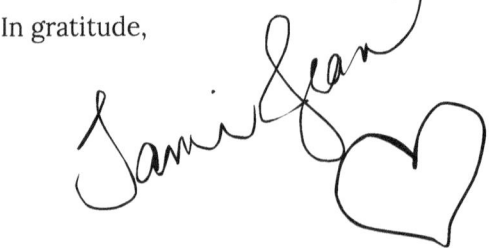

About the Author

Tami Jean grew up on Route 66 in the Mojave Desert in Barstow, California, until she was 13 ½ years old. She moved to Pennsylvania with her father after her parents' divorce. Her mother stayed in California. She often visits and loves the desert. She also loves the forests and landscape of Pennsylvania, where she lived with her father and grandparents. She attended Southern Lehigh High School in Coopersburg, Pennsylvania, with a brief transfer to Freedom High School during a turbulent time with her father. While in high school, Tami attended Lehigh Carbon Vocational School for Cosmetology, graduating from Allentown School of Cosmetology with her Manicuring License in 1992.

Soon after graduation from high school at age 19, Tami delivered her first son, Richard. While pregnant with her first son, Tami attended Southeastern Academy of Travel in Kissimmee, Florida, and received certification to work in the travel industry. This was not her passion, and she concurrently took a job as a nail technician after returning home. Tami's son Harley was born when she was 22 and her son Dalton was born when she was 24. Working in the beauty industry part-time while raising her three sons, she returned to Cosmetology School for her full Cosmetology License in 2001.

Tami was married in 1999 to her high school sweetheart and the father of her children, but their troubled marriage ended in 2008 in divorce. She soon met and married her second husband in 2011, which ended in separation in 2017 and divorce in 2019. Working in the Cosmetology field since 1993, along with many part-time supplemental jobs sprinkled in along the way, she was able to open her own salon in 2014 with her second husband. Closing that in 2019, she moved to be closer to her sons.

Throughout this process Tami was able to learn many valuable lessons, connect with many amazing women (and some men), and build her repertoire as a healer by taking many certifications, including Tarot Reading 1 and 2, The Art of Card Reading, Holy Fire Reiki 1 and 2, Astrology 101, Crystal and Advanced Crystal Healing, Folk Herbalism, and The Fundamentals of Trauma Certifications. These and many other learning opportunities sculpted Tami into the healer she is today.

Always wanting to learn, Tami is currently enrolled at Commonwealth Holistic Herbalism to earn her certification as a Family and Community Herbalist. After the death of her father-in-law in 2001 and the death of her first husband in 2023, both from ALS (Lou Gehrig's Disease), Tami also developed a passion for Holistic Medicine and natural remedies, with the goal of giving her sons and their families better alternatives for their health.

Founding Mending Hearts Healing in 2020, Tami has grown into a well-respected teacher, friend, daughter, lover, mother, and now grandmother of Miles James. She wears many hats, passionately bringing her plethora of tools together in the Heart Activation Toolkit program in hopes of reaching many women like herself who have suffered and survived verbal abuse.

To Learn More or Connect with Tami Jean